THE WED

The Wedding Day Book

Sue Dobson

ARROW BOOKS

Arrow Books Limited
62–65 Chandos Place, London WC2N 4NW

An imprint of Century Hutchinson Limited

London Melbourne Sydney Auckland
Johannesburg and agencies throughout
the world

First published 1981
Reprinted 1984
Revised edition 1989

Phototypeset by Input Typesetting Ltd, London
Printed and bound in Great Britain by
Anchor Press Ltd, Tiptree, Essex

ISBN 0 09 964960 8

Contents

	Introduction	7
1	Just the Two of You	9
2	The Engagement	12
3	Marriage and the Law	18
4	Making the Plans	29
5	Who Pays?	43
6	Cutting the Costs	45
7	Register Office Wedding	48
8	Second Marriages	54
9	Mixed Marriages	58
10	Choosing the Rings	62
11	Choosing the Music	79
12	The Flowers	86
13	The Photographer	101
14	Wedding Invitations	104
15	Choosing a Wedding Dress	118
16	Wedding Day Beauty	125
17	With a Little Bit of Luck	130
18	The Rehearsal	135
19	The Marriage Ceremony	137
20	The Bridesmaids	155
21	The Bridegroom's Role	160

22	The Best Man	164
23	The Ushers	169
24	The Reception	171
25	Wedding Presents	190
26	On the Day – Some Thoughts for the Bride	202
27	The Perfect Wedding Guest	205
28	The Bride's Parents	208
29	The Groom's Parents	211
30	When Parents are Divorced	214
31	Making a Speech	216
32	Thank-you Presents	225
33	Changing Your Name	228
34	Contraception – A Simple Guide	230
35	The Honeymoon	236
36	The Changing Times	241
37	The Bride's A–Z of Her Wedding	247
	Appendix I Countdown to Your Wedding	255
	Appendix II Arrangement Planner	260
	Appendix III Your Wedding Budget Planner	280

Introduction

A wedding is a momentous and very special occasion that brings together so many people, especially in the preparations for the great day. Which is why this book is written for everyone involved in the organizing of a wedding. It is the bride's – and her groom's – day and they are centre stage, so everything should revolve around their wishes; but without the help and support of their families and friends the job of creating a beautiful and memorable occasion would be much more difficult.

Every wedding, however similar in format, is different, as every couple will bring their own ideas and individuality to the proceedings. Although I have drawn on many of the traditional ways of getting married, I have also shown adaptations. While we can use tradition as a secure base from which to plan, the joy of a wedding today is that it can encompass the bride's own wishes and express her tastes and personality. A wedding can be what you wish it to be.

The aim of this book is to be a realistic, practical and informative guide. I can't promise to offer all the answers to every intricacy of the wedding day but I hope just about all the information you need will be found here.

Sue Dobson

1

Just the Two of You

Marriage is the most creative step you are ever likely to take. It entails a whole new way of thinking, living and loving. So it's a good idea to think hard about the future before rushing off to the altar or register office.

The first flush of romantic love is wonderful, but unless it leads on to a deeper, more enduring relationship, it will disappear all too quickly. The western image of love as an essential ingredient for marriage is not one that is accepted throughout the world. In many societies marriages are arranged by parents, who take into account family, money, class, occupation and other factors in deciding whether a couple may be suited. While we are not forced into the decision of whether to 'marry the person you love – or love the person you marry', the belief that love will conquer all tends not to be true in the long term. Couples with very disparate backgrounds often have a much tougher time in keeping a relationship together because of differing life experiences.

We demand a lot of each other in today's marriages, and with so many people living and working far away from parents and family it is easy to feel isolated, leaning heavily on one's partner for all one's needs. Roles are no longer clearly defined, which can be confusing. Divorce is easier – but neither easy nor painless. For a marriage to survive and survive happily in our ever-changing world and society, we have to learn to communicate, understand, show caring and work hard at living together amicably.

The old adage 'Marry in haste, repent at leisure' probably refers to not spending enough time together before marriage and not learning enough about each other. During the engagement period you should both have time to answer a few, but very important questions, like:

What do you expect from marriage?

Can you talk to each other about things that are important to you? Can you listen?

Are you in agreement about having, or not having, children?

Do you really like each other? The funny thing about love is that you can be head over heels infatuated with an exterior package and not like what's inside!

Do you respect each other's views, abilities, needs?

Do you really know them?

Is your future partner a good friend? Friends are people you can rely on and share with; laugh and cry with; who will understand and help you deal with the boring or unhappy parts of life.

Can you cope in the long term with the other person's annoying habits? Everyone has them!

Can you talk about sex – your needs and his?

Can you talk about money, and are you in general agreement about saving and spending priorities?

How well do you get on with each other's parents, and how closely will you be involved with them?

These are important things to think about because they will affect your future life together. Everyone has his or her idea of the ideal marriage, but every couple getting married is about to create something new and different – probably influenced by the relationship in marriage that their parents had, but still different.

A longer engagement gives you more time to think and to plan – both for the wedding itself and the future. It is a time for exchanging ideas, for listening to each other's views and needs, for making joint decisions, and for deciding that you really are going to be able to live with each other for a very long time.

2

The Engagement

Your engagement is a public expression of your love and intention to marry. You are a couple. The engagement may be long or short, but whatever its length it is a time for getting to know each other better and planning together for the future. This is also the time for making all the wedding arrangements. Do share your thoughts and ideas for the wedding day – each of you will have preferences and decisions made together will make the day even more special and enjoyable.

If your families have not met, arrange a meeting as soon as possible.

Announcements

The first people to be told should be both sets of parents. The days of chaperoning, of a man asking permission to 'pay court' and the girl's father being asked for his daughter's 'hand in marriage' are long, long gone, but parents are still concerned for their offspring's welfare and happiness. Because marriages affect family relationships, parents and close relatives like to be the first to know, then close friends, and eventually all acquaintances. It would be nice to appear at parents' homes to announce plans, bearing a bottle of champagne. If they are too far away, telephone them, but send them a bottle by post, through one of the many specialist mail order companies.

If both sets of parents have already met, this is the time for a small family celebration, at home or with a special meal at a favourite restaurant.

News can be shared with friends in all the traditional ways, also less conventionally – up in lights at a football stadium, on balloons, on a banner attached to the tail of a light aircraft or via a giant 'telegram' hung across the office. You can be as creative as you like in getting the message across!

An engagement can be announced formally or by personal letters, printed cards, in press announcements, or a combination of all three. Patterned writing paper or bought cards can be sent to far-flung relatives and friends. Newspapers, national and local, carry personal columns and announcement pages. Contact them for details of lineage rates and deadlines.

The engagement announcement in the press traditionally comes from the girl's parents. Many newspapers have printed forms to be completed, but a typical press announcement might read:

> The engagement is announced between Richard Blank, son of Mr and Mrs G Blank of Solihull and Janet Dash, daughter of Mr and Mrs L Dash of Birmingham

or

> Mr R A Blank
> and Miss J P Dash

The engagement is announced between Richard Anthony, only son of Mr and Mrs G R Blank of Solihull and Janet Patricia, eldest daughter of Mr and Mrs L C Dash of Birmingham

When parents are divorced, separated, or have remarried, both names and whereabouts can be stated. For example:

The engagement is announced between Richard Anthony, only son of Mr Graham Blank of Solihull and Mrs John White of Dover, Kent . . .

If one parent has died, the wording is:

. . . son/daughter of the late Mr G Blank and of Mrs M Blank . . .

With a very short engagement, the wording may be:

A marriage has been arranged and will shortly take place between Richard, only son of Mr and Mrs G Blank of Solihull and Janet, daughter of Mr and Mrs L Dash of Birmingham

Every newspaper has its own style of wording for announcements, so take a look at a copy beforehand and provide the necessary information either clearly handwritten or typed. Include a daytime telephone number as well as your full address – some newspapers like to check that the announcement is genuine. Most will accept copy for announcements by telephone. Have all the relevant information written out in front of you when you phone so you don't forget anything.

A party

Another way of announcing and celebrating your engagement is to throw a party. If the party is a way of announcing your news it may be as well to warn your parents and close family first, but make it a big surprise for your friends. Otherwise, use the party as a way of getting your friends together and celebrating your hopes for the future.

Such a party need not be elaborate or expensive but you could bring out a few bottles of champagne or sparkling white wine when the reason for the get-together is finally divulged. If the engagement has been announced and the reason for the party is clearly stated, your guests will probably bring along a small present and are likely to expect some good food as well as plenty to celebrate with!

Often the parents of a couple wish to throw a party. If they live long distances apart, you may end up having two parties as both sets of parents may wish to introduce you to members of the family and their circle of friends.

Incidentally, traditional etiquette demands that one only congratulates the man – expressing good wishes to the woman, never congratulations, on her engagement or marriage – but only the very formal would take note of that tradition now.

Presents

Some couples decide they'd rather dispense with the engagement ring and simply give each other a small present. Choose something personal and permanent.

Inexpensive ideas include cufflinks for him, ear-rings for her, a beautifully framed photograph, a record album, a chess set.

If someone sends you an engagement present, write a thank-you note immediately. News about your wedding plans would be appreciated.

Photographs

Some photographic studios will do an engagement portrait for free if you book them for the wedding photography. Ask around.

Unofficial engagements

If you are dispensing with the conventional engagement and simply getting married, tell both families and friends, celebrate with them in any way you wish and just send out the wedding invitations.

Breaking it off

If you've got engaged and made the announcements, then changed your minds and cancelled the wedding, everyone must be told. Traditionally the woman is supposed to return the ring, but this is seldom done now, unless it was a family heirloom. All gifts received from friends as a result of the proposed wedding should be returned, although the givers may suggest that you keep them. A press announcement, if made, should simply state:

16

THE ENGAGEMENT

The marriage arranged between Richard Blank and Janet Dash will not now take place

When gifts have been exchanged during a relationship, what you keep or give back to each other on the ending of the engagement should be decided between you – as amicably as possible.

3

Marriage and the Law

England and Wales

There are certain legal formalities that have to be complied with before a wedding ceremony, civil or religious, can take place.

To marry, by law both parties:

(a) Must be over the age of sixteen. If either of the parties is over sixteen but under eighteen, his or her parental consent must be given in writing.
(b) Must not be closely related to each other.
(c) Cannot already be married.
(d) Must be of sufficiently sound mind to be able to understand the nature of the contract of marriage.
(e) Must be acting freely and under no fear or duress.
(f) Must be of the opposite sex.

There are prohibited degrees of kindred and affinity – people who cannot marry because they are related – on the statute books, and if you are in any doubt you should check the list at the Superintendent Registrar's office. The Roman Catholic Church's list

18

extends well beyond that, and the Church of England has some which extend slightly beyond those prohibited by statute.

There is no legal reason why divorced people cannot re-marry, but the Superintendent Registrar will want proof that there is no legal barrier to a second marriage. This may be in the form of a death certificate or a decree absolute. The Anglican and Roman Catholic Churches regard marriage as permanent and will not generally marry divorcees in their churches. Some of the Non-Conformist churches are less rigid in their attitudes to divorced people.

There can be no such thing as a 'private' marriage or 'secret' wedding. Notice has to be publicly given and weddings must take place 'with open doors' – i.e. be public.

If the couple fulfil the legal qualifications they can apply to be married:

(a) in accordance with the rites of the Church of England;
(b) in accordance with the rites of any other religious denomination;
(c) before a Superintendent Registrar of Marriages in accordance with the Civil Law and without any religious service.

The ceremony must take place in the Office of a Superintendent Registrar, in a parish church of the Church of England or in a chapel or building registered as a place of worship. The marriage may only be solemnized between 8 a.m. and 6 p.m.

A marriage may, however, be solemnized at any time or place:

(a) pursuant to a Registrar General's licence;
(b) pursuant to a special licence of the Archbishop of Canterbury; or
(c) according to the usages of the Quakers and Jews.

There are four ways of authorizing marriage according to the rites of the Church of England, by:

(a) banns (the most popular);
(b) common licence;
(c) special licence;
(d) certificate issued by a Superintendent Registrar of Marriage.

Those wishing to be married in an Anglican church are usually expected to be members of the church or at least to have been baptized into the Church of England. The marriage must take place in the parish in which one (or both) member(s) of the couple live(s). If the couple live in different parishes the parish church of the bride is traditionally chosen for the wedding but this is custom, not law.

If the couple are members of a parish church outside of their home parish they can be married there as long as they are on the electoral roll. They should have been worshipping regularly at the church for at least six months.

The most usual procedure is marriage by *banns* – the reading of the banns in church on three successive Sundays. If the couple live in separate parishes, banns must be read in each of their respective parish churches and a certificate issued by the clergyman in the parish which is not the venue of the wedding certifying that the banns have been published there and no valid objection to the marriage has been received. There is no minimum residential qualification for Marriage by Banns, but this method will involve a minimum waiting period of fifteen days.

The marriage can take place on any day within the next three months after the banns have been published and between the times of 8 a.m. and 6 p.m.

Marriage by *Common Licence* (or *Ordinary Licence*) is a much quicker procedure but the residential qualifications are different. Only one of the couple need live in the parish where the marriage is to be celebrated, but must have been there for at least fifteen days immediately prior to the application. Only one clear day's notice need be given and the ceremony may take place at any time within the three months following the granting of the licence. Application for a licence should be made (in person) to the Surrogate for granting marriage licences in the diocese, who may be the clergyman at the chosen parish church, or to the Faculty Office, 1 The Sanctuary, Westminster, London SW1.

The man or woman making the application for a Common Licence is required to personally sign a declaration, an oath, stating that (a) there is no legal reason why the marriage cannot properly take place and (b) either the man or woman have lived in the district served by the church to be used for the ceremony for at least fifteen days prior to the application.

Marriage by *Special Licence* is an unusual form and the Archbishop of Canterbury only grants a Special Licence in unusual circumstances or in an emergency. The usual rules about residence and place and time of the ceremony are waived.

A *certificate* can be issued by a Superintendent Registrar to authorize a marriage in an Anglican church and application should be made at least twenty-one days before the wedding. Residential requirements are that each of the parties should have been resident in their own district for no less than seven days. However, this method of authorization for a church wedding ceremony is seldom used and a Surrogate's licence is usually preferred.

If a marriage is to be solemnized in a Church of England church after publication of banns, and one of the couple is living in England and the other is a serving member of the Royal Navy at sea, the banns can be published during morning service on board that ship by the chaplain or, if there is no chaplain, by the captain. A certificate recording the fact that the banns have been published and no valid objections have been brought to notice must be given to the minister ashore who is to perform the wedding ceremony.

Except where the marriage is to take place according to the rites of the Church of England or Church in Wales, notice to a Superintendent Registrar is usually necessary before a wedding ceremony can take place. If you want a religious service of marriage in a church or chapel belonging to another denomination, it is best to go to see the minister of the church and discuss the legal requirements with him or her before visiting the local Superintendent Registrar.

There are three methods of getting married under *civil law* in a register office.

(a) by Certificate issued by the Superintendent Registrar;
(b) by Certificate and Licence issued by a Superintendent Registrar;
(c) by Licence issued by the Registrar General:

Certificate

(i) Both the man and woman must have lived in the district controlled by the registrar for at least seven days before the application to marry is made;

(ii) one of the couple must appear to make the declaration in person;

(iii) if the couple live in areas controlled by different registrars, they must each visit and make the declaration before their own district registrars, and have lived in those districts for seven days prior to the visit.

A form is completed, stating the names, addresses and ages of the parties wishing to be married, and the building in which the wedding is to take place. A declaration has to be signed which states there is no legal objection to the marriage, and if one or both parties is under eighteen, that consent of the parents has been given.

When the Superintendent Registrar is satisfied with the information given to him, he makes an entry in his notice book and after a waiting period of twenty-one clear days he will issue the certificate for the marriage. The ceremony can take place within three months following the entry in the notice book (i.e. not three months after the certificate is actually issued).

To marry by certificate, then, there is a seven-day residential requirement for both members of the couple and a waiting period of fifteen clear days before the wedding can take place.

Certificate and licence

A similar declaration has to be made to the Superintendent Registrar's office as for the Certificate, but the residence qualifications are different:

(i) only one of the parties is required to make the arrangements in person at the registrar's office;

(ii) one person must have lived in the district for fifteen days prior to the application;

(iii) the other member of the couple must be in the country or have their normal place of residence in England or Wales when notice is given but it is not necessary for separate notice to be given to his/her local Superintendent Registrar, even if the couple live in different areas.

When the Superintendent Registrar is satisfied with the information given to him, he will make the necessary entry in his notice book and after one clear day has passed (excluding Sundays, Christmas Day and Good Friday) he will issue the licence for marriage. The Licence is valid for three months.

To marry by Licence, then, there is a residential

qualification of fifteen days for one party at least but it involves a waiting period of only one whole day.

Registrar General's licence

This was introduced in 1971 and enables civil marriages to take place elsewhere than in a register office or registered building. There is no statutory waiting period and no residential qualification, but it is only issued in emergencies and under very unusual circumstances, such as when one of the parties to be married is seriously ill, not expected to recover, and cannot be moved.

At the wedding ceremony the valid certificate or licence issued by the Superintendent Registrar(s) must be produced and the marriage must be witnessed by two other people – though they may be strangers to the couple and to each other.

Northern Ireland

Marriages may take place by any of the following methods: Licence, Special Licence, Banns, Certificate from a Registrar or Licence from a District Registrar of Marriage. The minimum legal age of marriage is sixteen but parental consent is required for those who wish to marry under the age of eighteen.

Scotland

The Marriage (Scotland) Act 1977 modernized the law on marriage in Scotland with the result that proclamation of banns in church is no longer acceptable as a legal preliminary to marriage, Sheriff's licences have been abolished and prior residence in Scotland is not a prerequisite for a legal marriage.

Regardless of where they live, any persons can marry in Scotland providing they:

- are at least sixteen years old;
- are not related to each other within the forbidden degrees of relationship;
- are unmarried (a previous marriage must have been ended by death, divorce or annulment);
- are not of the same sex;
- are capable of understanding the nature of a marriage ceremony;
- consent to the marriage;
- and providing that the marriage would be considered valid in any foreign country to which either member of the couple belongs.

A religious marriage may only be solemnized by a minister, clergyman, pastor, priest or other person entitled to do so under the Marriage (Scotland) Act 1977. A civil marriage can only be solemnized by a Registrar or Assistant Registrar who has been authorized to do so by the Registrar General. There are fewer restrictions in Scotland than in England and Wales regarding the place and time where a marriage can take place legally, but a civil wedding will normally be held in a Registrar's office during normal working hours. Two witnesses, aged sixteen or over, must be present at the wedding.

Each person wishing to be married has to obtain a marriage notice form (available from any registrar of births, deaths and marriages in Scotland) and give notice of intention to marry to the Registrar for the district in which the marriage ceremony is to take place. Notices should be submitted four to six weeks before the proposed date of marriage. The minimum notice period is fifteen days. Every person giving notice is required to sign a declaration to the effect that the information given is correct. As a safeguard against bigamous marriages a check is made on the information given, which is why a minimum of fifteen days' notice is required.

Together with the marriage notice it is necessary to supply the following documents:

(i) birth certificate;

(ii) in the case of a second or subsequent marriage, a copy of the decree of divorce (absolute or final) or annulment, or death certificate of former spouse;

(iii) if either party is domiciled outside the United Kingdom, a certificate of no impediment to marriage;

(iv) if any of these documents is in a language other than English, a certified translation has to be provided.

When he is satisfied there is no legal impediment to the marriage, the Registrar will prepare a Marriage Schedule. If the ceremony is to be a religious one, the Marriage Schedule will be issued to the couple (the prospective bride or groom must collect it in person) above seven days or less before the wedding day. This must be produced before the ceremony to the person performing the marriage. After the ceremony the Schedule must be signed by both parties, by the person performing the marriage and by the two witnesses, and returned to the Registrar within three days so he can register the marriage.

At a civil marriage the Registrar will keep the Schedule, having it available at the marriage ceremony for signature. Subsequently he will register the marriage.

4

Making the Plans
A Brief Guide

What sort of ceremony?

Once you've made the decision to marry, plans for the actual ceremony will begin to take shape. (And be warned – it will take longer and be much more tiring than you ever imagined!)

Firstly, decide on the type of wedding you both want – large or small, flamboyant or quiet – and where you want it to take place. Church or register office? Which one, and where?

You are lucky if such decisions come easily! Many a couple has started off wanting a quiet register office wedding and ended up having a big white wedding in church, with all the trimmings. Although it is your wedding, the families want to be involved, and many mothers want their daughters or sons to walk down the aisle beautifully dressed, and be the centre of admiration of family and friends, and for the wedding to be a grand occasion.

In some cases there are few alternatives. Where one or both of the couple have been divorced, for example, it is seldom possible to marry in Church of

England or Roman Catholic churches – but always check with your local Minister of Religion first. The Non-Conformist churches tend to be much more liberal about conducting weddings where one or both of the parties has been married before. If you are determined to have a church wedding ceremony it is usually possible to find a Minister who will conduct the ceremony, although neither the Minister nor the denomination may be your first choice.

When faced with this problem, many couples decide to have a civil wedding ceremony followed by a Service of Blessing in church. The Blessing is not a formal wedding ceremony but simply what its name implies: a blessing on the married couple. It is a short service and the bride is not expected to wear a traditional white dress or have bridesmaids. The bride and groom (who have already been legally married in a civil ceremony) together with a few close friends and relatives, meet in the church. The minister gives a brief address and prayers are said, followed by a gospel reading. Ask what his or her views are on the subjects of number of guests, flowers and music for the service.

Having decided on a possible date and on where you want the wedding to take place, go to see the Minister of Religion or local Superintendent Registrar to make sure that your chosen date is suitable. At popular times of year, especially in the summer months, dates, especially Saturdays, get booked up well in advance.

When seeing the Minister of Religion, ask him about the rules of his church. Will he allow confetti to be thrown, or photography inside the church?

Discuss music – will an organist or choir be available should you want them? What about bell ringing? Ask about fees. At this initial meeting, which is simply to introduce yourselves if you are not regular church-goers, and to make arrangements for the ceremony, you will probably not go into much detail.

It is a good idea to have several meetings with the person who is officiating at your wedding, get to know him or her a little, and share in some of the planning of the service. You will feel more involved if you have chosen the hymns and some of the readings. He will also want to talk with you about the relevance of a church wedding, and the bride will decide whether or not she wants to state in her vows, that she will 'obey' her husband. If you are of different religions it may be necessary for a meeting with clergy from both churches to make sure you each understand the other's beliefs. Should you have the opportunity of attending a marriage preparation course, do accept as they are usually relevant, worthwhile and helpful.

During this initial decision-making period you will have to decide on a budget for the wedding. Traditionally, the bride's father foots the bill for most things, but attitudes to this are changing and now most couples and their families share in the costs. So determine a budget between yourselves. If the groom's parents wish to contribute to costs, particularly the most expensive part of the day, the reception, the offer should come from them. It's best if both sets of parents have met by the time the wedding date is fixed and been able to talk about the arrangements. It is important that they should meet and communicate, for they are going to be linked with each other through the marriage of their respective children.

The reception

The next thing to decide on and book, as early as possible, is the reception. Will it be a lavish, sit-down meal, or a big buffet meal, or a finger buffet in the cocktail-party style? Roughly how many guests are you likely to have? Will you have a ballroom or marquee and book a caterer or will your family prepare all the food? Will you hold a reception at a local hotel or restaurant? What is your budget?

All these decisions have to be made well in advance because caterers, halls, and hotels get booked up very quickly. Some receptions may be booked even up to two years in advance!

Whether you decide on outside caterers or a local hotel or restaurant, you will need to visit them and decide on menus. They will offer you a selection of possible menus in a range of prices per head. Ask around local friends for advice on caterers and establishments with a good reputation. Get quotations from several, making sure you know what each includes. Make provisional bookings with a couple that you think are possible, and when you are more definite about numbers and have made a final choice on location, make a firm booking with one of them. Cancel any other provisional bookings.

Many couples now opt for a small reception or meal for close family to be held after the wedding ceremony and then a disco party in the evening for younger friends. If you plan to celebrate in this way, you will still need to book everything in advance.

The type of reception you hold, and the kind of food offered, will be affected by the time of day that you choose to marry, and whether the majority of guests will have travelled far to be at the ceremony.

The photographer

It is tempting to ask friends to take some pictures, since just about everyone owns a camera of some sort. However, unless you can count an aspiring David Bailey among the family or friends, it is advisable to book a local photographer and get some professional photographs done.

Your wedding photographs are a permanent reminder of your special day. You will look back on them in the years to come, and good professional photographs in an album will be much enjoyed. Your friends may produce some 'happy snaps', which will be fun, but there is always the risk that something could go wrong and you could be left with no photographs of your wedding.

Visit local photographers and ask to see their portfolios. Ask around friends, too, for recommendations. Photographers who specialize in wedding photography and portraits will have examples of their soft-focus romantic 'special effects' which can look very impressive. Again, ask for quotes, making sure you know exactly what is included in the prices quoted – for example, how many poses and prints will be offered to you, exactly where all the photography will take place, the type of album you will get and of course how soon after the wedding you will see the photographs.

Consider, too, having a videotape recording made of your wedding day. The cost is usually higher than for photographic prints. Sound recordings can also be made. You must check with the person officiating at the ceremony that they have no objections to filming or recording.

Once you've decided which photographer you like and who you think will do the best job, book him or her: again, comfortably in advance.

The florist

While you may not know exactly what flowers you will require, how many, or the size of your bouquet, it is advisable to book a florist well in advance. If you tell them roughly what you need, whether you want them simply to make a bouquet for you or whether you will require flowers for decorating the church and reception hall as well as the flowers for yourself and your bridesmaids, corsages for both mums and buttonholes for the men, they will have some indication of the time required to make up your order and can therefore tell you whether they will be able to accept the job or not.

Later, when you know much more about your plans, and have decided on the type of bouquet you want and whether the bridesmaids will be carrying posies, you can go into much greater detail and discussion with the florist, who should be good at offering ideas.

It is more sensible, and cheaper, to choose flowers

that are in season and readily available but if you are determined to have a particular exotic or out-of-season flower be sure to tell the florist well in advance, so enquiries can be made about whether it will be possible to get what you've set your heart on. Every florist has a horror story to tell of flowers ordered for a special day. Flowers being living things, they cannot always be grown to order or be flown in at a certain point in their development, timed to the day or moment.

Transport

White Rolls-Royces, kept specially for weddings, tend to be on the expensive side to hire. Hired cars for special occasions are not cheap, so the trend now is to have a special car for the bride and her father to arrive at the church, and for the newly married couple to go to the reception in. Often there is an additional hire car to take close family to the church and afterwards to the reception to ensure they arrive first. Otherwise, family and friends tend to use their own cars and to offer lifts to those without transport.

There are a variety of choices for transport, from white London cabs to Daimlers, vintage and veteran cars to horse-drawn carriages. The more complicated the travel arrangements, the earlier you need to start organizing them.

Check with out-of-town guests on how they will get to the wedding – they may need to be collected at the station or airport. They may also require accommodation. A helpful friend or usher may be asked to help if the family can't cope. If all overnighting guests are booked into the same hotel, transport could be arranged for them all to be collected and driven to the wedding.

Make sure each driver knows where he or she has to be, at what time, and is given the names of the passengers. Check on transportation after the reception, too. If you plan to leave on honeymoon in your car, someone will have to drive it to the reception venue.

Make sure your attendants have adequate transport for the whole day and check whether taxis are likely to be available for guests after the reception if they want them.

If the area around the church or reception venue has inadequate parking facilities it may be necessary to alert the local police to the potential problem or even have someone designated to direct guests to parking places.

Book hire cars well in advance, giving a likely estimate of the number and type of cars required and as soon as possible make a firm request for the exact number and where and when they will be needed.

Don't forget to check the details – white ribbons on the cars – and arrange for the best man to have money to tip the drivers.

The cake

As the cake is normally made by specialist bakers or family it is ordered separately. Place the order about four to six weeks before the wedding. Rich fruit cake tends to get better the longer it is kept – this is especially true of homemade cakes. So if you are thinking of making your own cake, or have had an offer from a friend or family member, it can be made at any time to suit the cook. Kept wrapped in foil and fed from time to time with a little brandy, it can be iced nearer to the wedding date.

Many people can make cakes; it's the icing of them that usually causes the difficulties. Some bakers and confectioners will professionally ice a homemade cake, so make enquiries locally to see if this service is available.

The size of the cake required will depend on how many guests are expected at the reception, how many pieces will be sent in boxes to those who cannot attend and whether you want to be traditional and keep the small top tier for use much later as a christening cake. Also, if you are having a small reception but planning a disco or future party at home, you might like to have some cake left over to serve then.

Wedding stationery

Stationery requirements include invitations and envelopes, reply cards, order of service sheets for the church, and menu cards, place cards, serviettes, cake boxes and personalized matchbooks for the reception. Matching writing paper is often available, otherwise attractive writing paper or packets of thank-you cards can be bought for acknowledging and thanking people for wedding presents.

Visit a local stationer and ask to see samples of printed stationery. Traditionally, wedding invitations were always engraved and consisted of a double sheet of good quality white or cream paper, engraved in black script. Today, single cards printed in black or silver are most popular and while engraved invitations are still used, they are much more expensive. When ordering, remember you will not need the same number as there are guests – one card covers all members of a family – but always order a few more than you think will be necessary. Ask for a proof so you can check that all the details are correct – spelling, punctuation, wording, names, addresses, dates and times. Return the proof with any corrections plainly and clearly made. Confirm the number required, the price agreed and the delivery date.

Send the invitations out about six weeks before the wedding date. Keep a list of those invited, and in columns next to the names leave space for ticking off their acceptance, if a gift has been received and whether the gift has been acknowledged. Don't forget that far-away friends and relatives who cannot travel to the wedding would probably appreciate an invitation as a memento of this important day.

Once the mums in both families have got together to decide on a guest list, try to stick to it as much as possible. If letters of good wishes and presents come from people who haven't been invited, write back and thank them, adding that you hope they will come to see you in your new home. If the guest list is very limited because of your budget and the high cost of a reception, you can always have an informal party at home after the wedding and honeymoon and invite all those you would like to have invited to the reception but couldn't, for whatever reason.

People understand that there is a limit to the number of guests that can be invited.

Place cards, serviettes and personalized match-books can be ordered ahead of time and will include the bride and groom's given names and the date of the wedding. (Order more matches than you actually need; they are good mementoes to hand out to friends.) Choice of designs and typefaces can be seen at the stationer's. Visit several and get quotations from each of them. If you are planning to include a route map or parking instructions with the invitations, consider whether to have these printed or, if only a few are required, you may wish to have them photocopied.

Order of Service sheets, to be given out at the church, can be ordered as soon as you have talked to the Minister and decided on the form of service and hymns to be sung. Some Ministers have strong feelings about the design, content and look of Order of Service sheets, so don't order yours until you have consulted him on the matter. He will be able to show you examples from previous weddings in his church.

Order of Service sheets can be one sheet of paper folded in half, or run to several pages. All that is required is the words of all the verses of the hymns to be sung, some prayers, names of anthems and responses, but some people like the entire ceremony to be printed (it is, of course, much more expensive to do this). On the front of the sheet the initials or names of the bride (in the bottom left hand corner) and groom (bottom right hand corner), the name of the church and the day, date and time of the wedding service are all printed. Order one sheet for every guest and a few spares. Again, distant relatives and friends may like to receive such a memento.

Choosing your helpers

If you are having a church wedding you will have to decide on whether or not to have bridesmaids, who will be asked to be best man and who will act as ushers. Bridesmaids are not usual at a register office, but a close friend or sister is usually asked to help the bride choose her dress and simply be around to give her moral support. A young child in the family, not wishing to be left out, may be asked to join the wedding group and wear a special 'party' dress for the occasion.

Bridesmaids are usually chosen from the bride and groom's family if they have younger sisters. If the woman chosen as chief bridesmaid is married, she is known as Matron of Honour. If neither of the families can provide a suitable person to be bridesmaid, then a close friend of the bride can be asked. Small brides-maids, flower girls or pageboys can look very pretty, but can also be a handful! If young children are to be included in the ceremony, an older girl is usually chosen as chief bridesmaid to keep an eye on them.

Incidentally, the person playing the role of 'best man' doesn't have to be a man! There have been lots of occasions where the best man has been a woman. Whoever is chosen has to be a good organizer and be reliable.

Announcing the wedding

If the engagement has been announced in a local or national newspaper, it follows that the wedding date will also be announced in the same way. Even if the engagement has not been formally announced, or if the couple have not been formally engaged, many people like to announce their forthcoming weddings in the paper. This should be done just before the actual date.

Again, check the usual form, wording and lineage rates used by the newspaper. A suitable wording might be:

> Blank-Dash: The marriage arranged between Mr Richard Blank and Miss Angela Dash will take place at St Mary's Church, Solihull on Saturday, June 15 at 3 p.m. Friends welcome at the church.

Should you want a photograph and account of your wedding to appear in the local paper check with the newspaper office as to what they require from you. Sometimes a reporter will come to the wedding, but mostly they are likely to ask you to complete a form and hand in or post a photograph of the bride and groom taken at the wedding. Give them at least a week's notice, preferably more, and they will tell you if they can send a reporter and/or photographer.

The honeymoon

Collect all the brochures you can find, come to an agreed decision on where you both want to go, how much you can afford, and the type of holiday you both want – lazing in the sun, exploring the countryside, in Britain or abroad, a big hotel or quiet family *pensione*. Book with a travel agent as soon as you've made the decision – and as early as possible.

Package holidays are often cheaper if you go on a weekday, and Saturday travel anywhere in the summer season is miserable, overcrowded and liable to delays. If you are planning a honeymoon out of Britain and having a summer wedding, or getting married on a date near a public or popular holiday time, consider staying fairly locally for a couple of days. With all the excitement of the wedding day you are likely to be tired anyway, and doing battle with crowded trains and airports is not conducive to good temper. If you stay in a cosy hotel in Britain for a few days then go abroad when you are feeling more relaxed you are likely to enjoy your honeymoon much more.

5

Who Pays?

The very high costs involved in a full white wedding and big reception, combined with the fact that many couples are working when they marry, have done much to change attitudes about who bears the cost of it all. The conventional pattern is that the bride's family organizes and pays for the wedding, but costs are now being shared between the bride and groom's family and the couple themselves.

Traditionally, the bride's father pays for the cost of press announcements, the bride's dress and the bridesmaid's dresses, flowers for the church and reception, photographers' fees, most of the transport, wedding stationery and the reception itself.

The groom pays for the hire, or cost, of his own clothes, for all costs at the church (minister's fees, licence, organist, choir and bell ringers' fees) except the flowers for church decoration. He pays for bouquets for the bride and her attendants, flower sprays for both mothers, buttonholes for himself, his best man and the ushers, the engagement and wedding rings, presents for the attendants and best man, transport for himself and the best man to the church and for himself and his bride to the reception; and for the honeymoon.

However, most people split costs in the way it suits them best. Typically, the bride will buy her own dress, and possibly those of the bridesmaids, particularly if she wants the style of dresses that are unlikely to be worn again. In many cases the bridesmaids buy their own dresses, or if small children, their parents buy them with an eye to the children using them as party dresses for wear after the wedding. The ushers will pay for the hire of their suits. The bride and groom themselves are likely to pay for the press announcements and help with the cost of wedding stationery and postage, also the photography. The bride will also probably share with her fiancé the costs of presents for attendants and best man.

Both families will now share the cost of the reception, which is usually the main expense of the day, and the groom's family are also likely to share the cost of decorating the church and reception with flowers.

Few men are likely to be able to pay for the entire honeymoon and most working women want to contribute to this in the way they would for any holiday.

6

Cutting the Costs

A wedding is a very special occasion – it is also a very expensive one. How much you choose to spend is, obviously, up to you and your family, but there are ways to save and cut costs without ruining the whole day.

A beautiful wedding dress can cost the earth – but you can hire it for the cost of a cheap new one. Alternatively, you can buy at sale time, make your own dress from a pattern or send for a cut-out, ready-to-sew dress.

It is sometimes possible to hire bridesmaids' dresses, and usually possible to hire pageboy attire. Bridesmaids are often happy to pay for their own dresses – especially if they can be worn again on future occasions.

If you hire a dress, you will be able to hire a veil and headdress, which is cheaper than buying them. Alternatively you could wear a short veil instead of a long one, or wear a juliet cap or pillbox hat, with or without a small veil attached.

Hire cars for a big wedding can be pretty expensive. The answer is to hire one to take the bride and her father to church and the newly married couple to the reception. For the rest, enlist friends and their cars.

Good photographs of the wedding will be appreciated in the future and it could be false economy to rely on friends with instant cameras. Cut costs when using a professional by ordering an ordinary album rather than a deluxe version, or if you have a friend who is really talented he or she may do the photographs as a wedding present.

Flowers are an essential part of a wedding and the church and reception hall look so much more attractive when decorated. The expensive way is to have all the arrangements done by a florist, but there are sure to be friends or family who would be delighted to help decorate with flowers. Some florists will give a discount on boxes of flowers when the bride's bouquet is ordered from them, but it is not essential to buy expensive blooms from a florist. If you live near a large wholesale flower market you may be able to buy favourite blooms by the box. Or find friends with gardens and window boxes who will be proud to denude them for such an important occasion! Tables at the reception can be decorated prettily and inexpensively with small posy bowls.

You can have engraved invitation cards and printed service sheets – or buy ready printed cards and use duplicated service sheets plus hymn books. For a small wedding, write your own invitations on attractive paper.

The reception is usually the most expensive part of the wedding day. At the top end you can have a large guest list at the reception in a big hotel with a posh sit-down meal and champagne flowing freely.

Less expensive alternatives are to hire caterers and a hall, invite fewer guests, or do the catering yourself (and rope in plenty of friends). A small family meal plus a disco for many is usually cheaper – and can be more fun – than a formal reception. Limiting the choice of alcohol on offer cuts costs. One way of hinting subtly that the guests might stop drinking soon is for the bride and groom to leave the reception early! You can also have an agreed time limit for 'free' drinks, after which a pay bar comes into operation.

If you are organizing the reception and buying the drinks ask around all the off-licences in the district to see if they will give a big discount on a large order. It is not necessary to have champagne at a wedding – a sparkling wine is perfectly acceptable. Having only one type of drink available (plus some non-alcoholic drinks) cuts down the expense and simplifies the ordering.

A reception is a time to be creative: why not have a picnic, or a tea reception for an afternoon wedding – scones, fresh fruit jam and cream; a real wedding breakfast – kedgeree and sparkling wine or champagne with orange juice? The cake could be three-tiered and ornately decorated, but equally could have one or two tiers and be homemade (another wedding present from a friend?). A homemade cake can always be professionally iced.

A wedding can still be impressive however simple, when some thought and ingenuity are injected. Friends will be pleased to have their skills recognized and happy to give their time as recognition of their friendship. A wedding where everyone contributes will be a happy one.

7

Register Office Wedding

Many people choose to have a civil ceremony because they think it is the quickest and quietest way to be married or because a religious ceremony in church would have no meaning for them. Others marry in a register office because they do not share the same religious beliefs, do not have their parents' support for the marriage, want to marry without pomp or ceremony, or because one or both may be divorced and unable to remarry in church. On average, about half the number of weddings that take place in Britain every year are held at register offices.

There are two forms of marriage document issued by a Superintendent Registrar for a secular ceremony – a Certificate and a Licence.

Marriage by certificate

The bride or groom must go in person to the Superintendent Registrar in their area to give notice of the intended marriage. Relevant forms and declarations are completed. Both parties to the marriage must have lived in the district in which they are to be married for seven days prior to the application. If they live in separate districts, notice must be given in both the bride and groom's home districts. The Superintendent Registrar enters the notice of marriage in his book, and after twenty-one clear days have elapsed, and there is no impediment, he issues the certificate for the marriage. The wedding must take place, in the building specified on the certificate, within three calendar months from the date of entry (not three months from the date of issuance of the certificate).

Marriage by licence

This requires the same legal declarations, but only one person must have lived in the district in which the wedding is to take place for the preceding fifteen days. The other party to the marriage must be in or normally live in England or Wales when notice is given but does not have to be in the district at the time nor does he or she have to make a declaration before his or her own local Superintendent Registrar. The licence to marry will be issued when one clear day has elapsed after giving the notice (not including Sundays, Good Friday or Christmas Day). The notice to marry is valid for three months only. As with the Certificate, the wedding must take place between 8 a.m. and 6 p.m. in the district where the notice was given. Remember that many register offices are only open until 12 noon on Saturdays.

Who to invite?

When you first go to visit the registrar, you can ask him or her how many people can be invited to the ceremony. Some register offices are small, some can accommodate about twenty people, others are very much larger. Even if the office can accommodate a lot of guests, bear in mind that the ceremony is short (about 10 to 15 minutes) and there is likely to be a ceremony before yours and one after – at busy times of the year, weddings can be booked every twenty minutes. Trying to get together with a large number of people from several weddings including your own can become confusing, not to mention overcrowded. So it is wise to keep the numbers to a minimum. Photography is not usually permitted during the ceremony.

The ceremony

On the day of the wedding, the bride and groom, two witnesses, close family and guests meet at the register office, preferably about ten minutes before the ceremony is due to start. At the ceremony the marriage official usually makes a short introductory address to the couple. The bride and groom declare that there is no lawful impediment to the marriage, and call on the attending guests to witness the marriage. They join hands and speak the words that form the legal contract of marriage, then exchange rings. The couple are asked to sign the register, then the two witnesses sign it.

The reception

This can be similar to the type held after a church wedding. If the ceremony takes place around lunchtime, the newly married couple, their close family, witnesses and a few friends may decide to go to a restaurant for a celebratory meal. In the evening, (or later perhaps even after the honeymoon) they may hold a party or disco for all the friends who were unable to be at the ceremony. There may be a wedding cake and a toast to the bride and groom's happiness at such a party.

Others prefer to invite everyone back to their home for a celebration breakfast or brunch, which may have been prepared by friends, family or outside caterers. A full reception such as that normally associated with a big white wedding could also be held.

What to wear

What to wear is a question of personal choice as there are no strict conventions as to dress at a register office wedding. Some brides choose to have a formal white wedding dress, but bear in mind that a dress with a long train was designed for a church where there is plenty of space, which few register offices have. A wedding is a good excuse to indulge and buy a pure silk or designer dress or suit, for a civil ceremony lends itself to the wearing of something that could be worn again on other occasions, which the traditional wedding dress seldom does.

Buy the outfit well ahead of time so there is no last minute rush to find suitable accessories. The best shoes and handbag you can afford will be a good investment for future use. A well-cut suit or dress with a coat or jacket are classics that won't make the wedding photographs look dated after a year or two.

A hat is not essential for a civil wedding, but if you like them and look good in them, choose one that doesn't hide your face – from your husband or the photographer!

As for a traditional white wedding dress, the right underwear is essential – a seamless bra and full length petticoat under fine silk, for example.

Large bouquets tend to look out of place at a civil wedding, so a corsage, a single orchid or small posy can be chosen. The groom's buttonhole flower and the buttonholes and corsages of the guests should tone with the colours of the bride's chosen flowers.

The groom should choose his clothes for the ceremony just as carefully as the bride. Quite often it is the groom who wears white! A white suit with tie and buttonhole flower in a shade that matches the bride's suit or picks out a colour from her dress looks very effective.

If the small group of people who will be at the wedding get together before the day and discuss what they will be wearing, they can also tone in with the general colour scheme chosen by the bride and groom. The overall effect of carefully thought-out colour scheming will be well rewarded when seen in the wedding photographs.

A bridesmaid is not necessary at a register office wedding, but a favourite child or younger sister will enjoy dressing up for the day and carrying a posy. The colour of her dress should blend with that of the bride. Both mums should wear smart outfits that tone together. Hats for the mothers are optional depending on whether they feel comfortable in them.

As there are no strict conventions for dress at a

register office wedding it is a case of 'anything goes' and personal taste and choice. This can mean a long or short dress for the bride, in white or a favourite colour, with or without a hat, with or without flowers. The man may be as formal or informal as he likes, though it is more usual for him to wear a formal suit with buttonhole. It is complimentary to his future wife if he takes as much care over his clothing as she does over hers.

8

Second Marriages

A second wedding ceremony needn't mean quietly sloping off to the register office with just a few close friends – unless you want to, in which case you probably wouldn't be reading this book! Most people getting married for the second time are even more determined that this time it will be 'for keeps' and want their wedding to be a special occasion.

When it's second time around for both parties, the main difference in the wedding day happenings is that they are usually less formal and more relaxed than for a first wedding. For the actual ceremonies and legal formalities for a wedding, see the relevant chapters elsewhere in the book.

The clothes Wear whatever suits you – something special, but there are no rules. Most people feel it is inappropriate to wear full white bridal dress but some women who didn't wear it first time around choose to do so for their second weddings. Many clergy will not accept bridal white for a Service of Blessing, so check first.

A silk suit or dress is always elegant and acceptable. As to colour, wear whatever you look good in. A bow, some jewellery or small hat are all suitable headgear – a big floppy hat is likely to hide too much of your face for the photographs. Choose leather or good new accessories to complete an elegant look.

The groom should dress to suit his bride's outfit and can wear morning dress, business-style suit or lounge suit.

Flowers A corsage or small posy is usually chosen.

Invitations Less formal, usually, but see the chapter on this subject.

The reception Different from the last time, preferably. Guests could get that *déjà vu* feeling. A wedding cake is not essential but go ahead and have one if you really like and want it. Unless parents particularly want to provide a reception it is usually the couple who are the hosts at the party. Some couples choose to take a few friends to a restaurant to celebrate after the ceremony, some to go to a hotel, others to have a cocktail party or throw a party later on at home. Celebrate in whatever way you choose and will enjoy most – there are fewer pressures from family and to please others second time around, so enjoy it.

The guests Some people seem to think former husbands, wives or lovers will enjoy coming to the wedding but it seems a bit insensitive, and bitterness has been known to creep through after a few drinks. Aunts, uncles and ex-in-laws are not ideal guests, either. It's better to invite mutual friends to a celebration and leave individual family and friends from past relationships to another time, and at home.

Children can be a problem. They are usually invited because the couple want their children from a previous marriage to be, and be seen to be, part of the new family unit. Older children, especially if they live with the ex-partner, may find their loyalties divided. If they don't want to come, have a small dinner party for them later and try to understand their dilemma without feeling hurt. When children are young and want to join in, make it a special day for them, include them in everything and make them feel important.

The speeches Keep them short – if you must have them. Avoid family speech-makers and choose those among your friends who are witty. It's probably better to stick simply to toasting the bride and groom.

The honeymoon Call it a holiday if you like, but take one. Make sure you leave your (and his) children behind. A married couple's first loyalty is to each other and that needs to be clear from the start. You deserve time alone together, a rest – and having a special holiday adds to the sense of occasion.

Second marriages in church

Widows and widowers may marry again in church or synagogue. If the bride is marrying for the first time she may wear what she wishes, as may the groom. If the bride is a widow, the general custom is for her to choose a special dress or suit and not to wear the traditional full white dress and veil of the young bride. However, she could choose a long, simply cut dress, perhaps in cream silk, and pillbox style hat with tiny veil attached or pretty picture hat if she wishes to come close to the traditional style. The groom can wear morning dress or, more informally, a lounge suit.

9

Mixed Marriages

The rigid rules that once held so many problems for Roman Catholics who wished to marry a non-Catholic partner in church have been much relaxed in the last few years. While the Catholic Church, like many others, still discourages mixed marriages, many dispensations are granted to Catholic/Protestant couples every day – in fact over 60 per cent of weddings held in Catholic churches are 'mixed marriages'.

Pope Paul VI did away with the rule that excommunicated Roman Catholics for marrying in non-Catholic ceremonies and in 1966 the celebration of mixed marriage 'with the sermon' was permitted. In 1970 he abandoned the necessity of written promises which stated that both parties agreed to the bringing up of any children from the marriage as Catholics. Instead, he said that the Catholic partner was 'gravely bound' to make a sincere promise that he or she would do all in their power to have the children baptized and brought up with the teachings of the Catholic Church. The non-Catholic party had to be informed of this promise, whether verbal or written. A year later the Anglican-Roman Catholic Commission on the Theology of Marriage and its Application to Mixed Marriages agreed that the duty to educate children in the Roman Catholic faith was 'circumscribed by other duties such as that of preserving the unity of the family'. What it all boiled down to was that each partner should respect the other's faith.

In 1977 the Roman Catholic bishops of England and Wales allowed parish priests to grant dispensations. This had previously been the prerogative of the bishops. Any couple of differing religions are expected to meet with a priest or minister of each faith and learn something of the other's religion. Ideally, there should be several meetings over a reasonably long period – some Catholic dioceses are requesting that at least six months' notice of the intended marriage should be given, to allow time for discussion and understanding of the importance of marriage.

The Catholic Church looks more favourably on a marriage between two baptized Christians. It considers marriage to be a sacrament and its views on the permanence of marriage remain unchanged – it is indissoluble. During the informal discussions with a priest, the Roman Catholic partner has to promise (verbally) to guard his or her faith and do all in his or her power to bring up any children as Catholics. If the priest is sure that the non-Catholic partner understands these promises, he will grant permission or dispensation for the couple to marry. However, he personally cannot refuse permission – if he wants to withhold the dispensation he must refer to his bishop, and the bishop may take it even higher for a decision.

While a Roman Catholic is expected to marry in a

Catholic church, it is possible for the wedding to take place in an Anglican church without the threat of excommunication. A dispensation for this is examined on an individual basis in England and Wales. The most usual reasons for granting such a dispensation are when the bride is a practising member of a particular church and is part of that church's community, so would have strong reasons for marrying in her parish church, or in cases where family unity would be jeopardized by the celebration of a wedding in a Catholic church. A priest or bishop would be less likely to agree for 'cosmetic' reasons, such as another church being considered prettier.

A mixed marriage can only take place in one church not in both. If it is to be held in a Church of England church then the vicar of that church must perform the actual marriage rite, though the Catholic partner's parish priest may participate if wished. Unfortunately, the two Churches do not yet share communion, so as one partner will not be able to participate, the marriage will usually take place without a Nuptial Mass or Eucharistic Service.

It is virtually impossible for a Jew to marry someone who is not of the Jewish faith in a religious ceremony in a synagogue, for Judaism does not accept the concept of mixed marriage.

There is seldom any problem with a marriage between people belonging to different Protestant and Non-Conformist denominations. It is acceptable for a Quaker to marry a non-member if he/she understands the faith and is in sympathy with it. Written recommendations from two full members are required.

There are serious problems for a Christian who wants to marry a non-Christian in a religious ceremony. The Catholic Church will not agree to hold the wedding and an Anglican minister will want to be very sure that the person understands and accepts the Christian faith before agreeing to officiate at such a ceremony.

10

Choosing the Rings

Rings have been worn as adornment for over 4000 years so when you go to the jeweller's to choose yours you are continuing an age-old tradition. An engagement and wedding ring is an outward symbol of love and commitment. The original circle of the wedding band, without beginning or end and enclosing the finger, symbolizes the full involvement of the wearer with the person who gave the ring. The ring you choose together, with all its symbolism and meaning, will be a permanent reminder of your commitment and love for each other.

Wedding rings can be bought in platinum, in white gold of 9-carat standard and 18-carat standard. In yellow gold you can buy 9-carat, 18-carat and 22-carat rings. The lower the number of carats the harder the metal and the cheaper it becomes. Only about a third of the metal in 9-carat gold rings is pure gold, the other part is made up by alloying the gold with copper, or in the case of white gold the alloying metal is often nickel. The purer the gold the greater lustre it will have and the more it will hold its value. As it is not possible to make an alloy of white 22-carat gold, if you want a white metal wedding ring of top quality you would buy 18-carat white gold or platinum.

The price of engagement rings can vary enormously – in fact the sky is the limit. At the lower end of the price scale, most engagement rings will be of 9-carat gold, and because stones such as sapphires are not as expensive as the same size in diamonds, coloured stones are often used for engagement rings and can be mixed with diamonds to make a very attractive ring.

When you visit the jeweller's and pick out some rings you like, ask to borrow the eye lens (Loupe) and look at the hallmark and the stones. They are called inclusions and all the coloured stones like sapphires, rubies, emeralds and so on will have them, as will diamonds. A hallmark is required by law to identify the maker of the article, what proportion of gold is contained in it and where and in what year it was tested by the Assay Office. Platinum is also hallmarked. Your jeweller can explain all the markings. Make sure you choose a reputable jeweller for this very important purchase. You will have ideas on the style of ring you want. Take your own colouring into account, also the shape of your hands. Long fingers can take bolder rings, plump fingers need simple designs, small hands require something dainty. Avoid rings that look as if they will catch or scratch. Very unusual or complicated settings may look good initially but may not be comfortable or convenient to wear all the time.

In the choosing of your wedding ring, which you will probably wear for the rest of your life, you can express your personality in many ways – through the hardness (9-carat gold) or softness (22-carat gold) of the metal, the colour of the metal (yellow or white or a combination of the two), the width of the ring and the design. For a ring made of gold, 18-carat is often recommended; this is the ideal proportion of gold to other metals for a craftsman to work into beautiful designs, for it to be hardwearing, have a good depth of richness and colour, and holds its value longer. There is a wide variety of widths and designs in wedding rings, as a glance at any jeweller's window will show. And they can be specially made to your own design – the bride and groom's names or a single message can be so neatly entwined that only you will know the ring's secret. A jewellery designer will probably want to meet and talk to you before he creates the ring for you.

Whether you choose a one-off design or a ready-made one, tell the jeweller what you like and dislike and the sort of ring you are searching for. That way he will be more able to help you choose. There are eight basic aspects of design to consider: whether you want a wide ring or a narrow one, a flat topped or stoned style, a smooth or textured surface or a diamond milled surface which has a faceted look, or a combination of surface finishes. Alternatively, you may choose to have a matching, interlocking engagement and wedding ring, which looks very attractive.

You may consider the idea of remodelling a ring that has been handed down through the family, but this is often a very expensive process. One way to avoid the excess cost but still incorporate an heirloom is to surround it with two very narrow bands, one worn above and one worn below the precious ring in a sort of sandwich with the old ring polished up. This has the same effect as a combination-style ring, a style which has its phases of popularity.

Consider, too, buying an antique ring as an engagement ring. Older jewellery is very attractive and can be bought at antique markets, or many jewellers have a selection.

Cost is obviously a factor when choosing a wedding ring, and the ever-rising gold price means that 22-carat is now often. beyond the pocket of most people. Remember, though, that this item on your shopping list is meant to outlast everything you buy, so buy the best you can afford.

When should you buy the ring? You need time to select this important purchase, so if you do plenty of 'window shopping' beforehand you can be more sure of the type and style you like most. Try to choose a day other than a Saturday, when shops are at their busiest, and avoid peak shopping periods like Christmas. Also, you may need a special style or size that is not in stock and has to be ordered. A ring to be specially designed will take several weeks before it is completed. Some jewellers will appreciate a phone call and an appointment so they can give you more time and help. Ideally, an engagement and wedding ring should be chosen together, to make sure they are of a similar colour and shape. They should fit closely together and not rub against each other.

Your fingers are affected by the climate – or even the time of day – so it is as well to bear this in mind when trying on rings. Often fingers are slightly larger in the afternoons, and of course in hot weather.

Under such conditions the ring should be a good fit and just a little bit tight. On a day when your hand is cold the ring should not fit too tightly. If the ring is very wide, the finger size will have to be a little larger.

The idea of exchanging rings has become very popular again and you may want to choose matching rings so symbolizing even further your unity as a married couple. There are many designs available – you simply have to make the choice. Another way of personalizing rings is to have a message engraved inside the ring(s) or simply the dates of the engagement and wedding inside each ring.

Birthstones

Gems were first worn by rulers to symbolize their divinity and position, and the first record we have of jewellery being worn was by an Egyptian queen, Zer, around 5500 BC. Precious stones were once believed to be dewdrops condensed and hardened by the sun and each held a meaning. The symbolism of the colours of the stones included white to mean life, joy and innocence; blue signified heaven, virtue and truth while green offered hope, faith and victory; purple brought suffering and sorrow, and yellow, God's goodness. Stones were also considered to be either male or female depending on their depth of colour. For example, a sapphire would be a female stone if a pale, sky-blue colour or a male stone if nearly indigo.

Coming a little closer to our own era, in Tudor times wedding rings included precious stones. These were ascribed with mythical significance by the Church of Rome: ruby meant glory, emerald gave tranquillity and happiness, a crystal meant simplicity and purity, a diamond showed invulnerable faith; with the sapphire came hope, with onyx, sincerity, and an amethyst showed humility. This endowment of stones with human properties was probably because our ancestors believed them to influence their fortunes – and misfortunes.

Birthstones are often chosen for setting in engagement rings. Gemstones are supposed to be a talisman with various meanings for the wearer, some of which are listed here. Sometimes the list of stones is applied to calendar months and sometimes to particular dates according to the signs of the zodiac.

AQUARIUS
January 20–February 19 – Garnet

A deep red-coloured stone, often found close to diamonds. It was fashionable in Ancient Egypt and in Victorian days, and is supposed to guard the wearer against poison, plague and lightning. It also represents truth, constancy and fidelity.

PISCES
February 20–March 20 – Amethyst

A purple stone, known and worn for at least thirty-four centuries. Bishops have a ceremonial ring containing amethyst and it speaks of sincerity, serenity, virtue and high ideals. It is also said to be a preventative against violent passions.

ARIES
March 21–April 20 – Aquamarine

This tone ranges in colour from a clear limpid water blue to a blue/green colour. It is a symbol of happiness, courage and everlasting youth.

TAURUS
April 21–May 20 – Diamond

Probably the most famous and coveted of stones – long before Marilyn was singing that they are a girl's best friend, people were aware of the value of diamonds. The Greek name Adamas means indomitable and legend has it that if given freely a diamond will bring luck. Until the fifteenth century only members of the aristocracy were allowed to wear them. Innocence, repentance and purity are symbolized in this stone, which is said to protect the wearer from evil.

GEMINI
May 21–June 20 – Emerald

A lovely green colour, and ideal for an engagement ring as it is said to bring true love, success, constancy, loyalty and true affection. It is also supposed to discover false friends and save you from drowning if you are a fisherman! Said to be Cleopatra's favourite stone, emerald was believed to have great healing powers, especially for painful eyes, and the peaceful green colour was associated with bringing peace and calm to anyone or anything that was troubled.

CANCER
June 21–July 20 – Pearl

A creamy white sphere that represents innocence, vitality, energy, health and beauty, though said by some to bring tears and therefore often not considered to be a suitable stone for an engagement ring – but it is said to bring wealth!

LEO
July 21–August 21 – Ruby

A rich red stone that has always been a symbol of great wealth. It is said to bring love and contentment – and also preserve chastity! The price of a virtuous woman is far above rubies, according to the Book of Proverbs.

VIRGO
August 22–September 22 – Peridot

Less famous perhaps than most of the birthstones, peridot is an unusual shade of green. It is believed to bring faithfulness and gladness, and also to cure an inferiority complex!

LIBRA
September 23–October 22 – Sapphire

Sapphires can be almost any colour, except red. Ideally they are a deep cornflower blue but more usually a very pale blue or dark greenish blue. This pure blue was supposed to symbolize heaven so popes and other religious leaders wore them a lot. The luckiest of all gems, the sapphire was sacred to Apollo and is said to bring peace, wisdom, virtue, and charm, as well as freeing the wearer from enchantment.

SCORPIO
October 23–November 22 – Opal

A fascinating milky-white stone with flashing reds and greens as it is moved about. There is a myth that it is unlucky, probably because it is brittle and shows changing colours so therefore it is often spurned. Yet it is a symbol of hope, faith, good fortune, romance and lasting love – though lucky only for Scorpios.

SAGITTARIUS
November 23–December 20 – Topaz

Often confused with yellow citrine which is much cheaper, the topaz is usually a pale yellowish/pinkish colour. Legend has it that it can ward off insomnia and asthma, though only around the time of a full moon. It symbolizes fidelity and friendship.

CAPRICORN
December 21–January 20 – Turquoise

A pale blue opaque stone that originates from Turkey. It was used in place of money in Tibet, and when you ride your horse there the turquoise will keep you safe! It is said to prevent arguments, bring great success and happiness plus prosperity in love.

The ring of history

The origin of betrothal and nuptial rings is said to date back to the caveman, when he bound his mate's wrists and ankles with plaited reeds or leather. As time went by only the wrists were tied until, still later, only the finger was bound. Another theory concerning the origins of the wedding ring is that it was the symbol of the bridegroom's purchasing power and that the betrothal ring could well have been given as a substitute for a dowry. There is an old Jewish custom of exchanging or giving something to ratify an agreement and it was a Roman practice to give a ring when concluding a bargain.

In the early days only the men wore gem-set rings and then as an ornament or token of power by those in important positions. It was the ancient Greeks who regarded the ring as a token of affection. Betrothal rings were generally regarded as being a prelude to marriage, though between the Vikings the giving of a ring was more as a token of memory than a binding agreement.

Rings were well established by Roman times. At the wedding feast the woman would be presented with a ring, less to denote her position of wife than as housekeeper, for this ring would bear a seal with which she was expected to seal up cupboards or wine jars.

Archaeological excavations have given us many insights into the lifestyles of the past. The ruins of Pompeii revealed love rings of gold, one bearing an engraving of a couple holding hands. It was a custom in Ancient Egypt to place a piece of ring-money (used before the introduction of coins) on the bride's finger to indicate that she was now endowed with her husband's wealth.

According to a Latin text, the ring's circular and endless shape shows that mutual affection and love will flow from one to another as in a never-ending circle – a symbolism that has survived through the centuries to present times.

Roman parents gave each daughter's fiancé a ring in token of their betrothal and the man presented a girl with a similar token of his pledge. These rings indicated the promise to marry but were not ultimately binding and the couple were free to break their engagement at any time before the actual wedding day.

Parents played a role in Anglo-Saxon times, too, for then it was usual for a boy and girl to be promised to each other in childhood. The boy's father gave the girl a ring to signify that she would marry his son when old enough. When the actual wedding took place, the betrothal ring was exchanged for the wedding ring, which would be gold and worn on the third finger of the right hand.

The fact that wedding and engagement rings are worn on the third finger of the left hand has a variety of beliefs and legends attached to it. The left hand was chosen for ornaments because it was used less by the majority of people. At the time of the Roman Empire Macrobius (about 400 AD) said that the thumb is too busy to be set apart, the forefinger is far too big and strong for such a romantic task, the little finger is too small and weak so the finger left to carry the matrimonial ring is the 'pronubus', the third finger. Then there was the 'medical' reason which Henry Swinburne wrote about in the seventeenth century. There was an ancient belief that a delicate nerve ran from the third finger straight to the heart, but seventeenth-century doctors believed they had traced a vein of blood, the *vena amoris*, from the third finger to the heart. So that was the 'love seat' of the finger destined to bear the ring.

There was a practical reason, too. Not only was the left hand used less than the right but the third finger was most protected. It was used least and was the only finger which could not be stretched out on its own, so a ring set on that finger was least likely to be damaged.

The Roman Catholic Church gave a different reason for the same custom when the wedding ceremony took place in church as part of the formal order of service, which included the placing of the ring on the finger. The thumb and the first two fingers represented the divine Trinity of Father, Son and Holy Spirit, while the third finger was symbolic of the humanity of God in Chirst, so that was the one considered most appropriate to carry the symbol of human love and fidelity. In 1549, the English Prayer Book specified that the marriage ring should be placed on the left hand.

There is evidence that the ring was sanctified by the Church from the eleventh century onwards. During the Reformation the ring became an essential part of the wedding ceremony and the betrothal ring was supplemented by the wedding ring. By the middle of the sixteenth century it was specified how the ring should figure in the religious ceremony. The priest was to place the ring on each of the fingers of the bride one by one, until it came to the ring finger, where he left it.

In 1837 an Act of Parliament was passed stating that a marriage could legally take place without a ring, but this idea does not seem to have been very popular, presumably because a wedding ring has too much history, sentimentalism and symbolism attached to it.

Although in Britain engagement rings are now worn on the third finger of the left hand, this was not always so. The second finger was once the one reserved for plighted troth. The sign language of ring placement indicated our forebears' marital status: if a man or woman was willing to marry but not actually betrothed a ring was worn on the index or forefinger of the left hand; if engaged, on the second finger; if married, on the third finger; and if wishing to remain single, then a ring was worn on the little finger. This non-verbal communication began to die out when strangers of the opposite sex began to mix more freely.

Posy, regard or motto rings have been exchanged by friends and lovers from the Middle Ages to quite recent times, being very popular during the reign of Queen Victoria. They were heavily engraved and inscribed with couplets such as 'In thee a flame, In me the same'. Sometimes they were set with gems, initial letters of the stones giving the message. Ruby, Emerald, Garnet, Amethyst, Ruby, Diamond. Or sometimes they spelt out the lady's name: Pearl, Emerald, Amethyst, Ruby, Lapis-Lazuli. Another favourite was to spell out the word 'dearest' in gems:

Diamond, Emerald, Amethyst, Ruby, Epidote, Sapphire, Turquoise. The use of the fiancé's birthstone in an engagement ring was said to bring luck, so presumably the ideal combination was a meaningful word that contained the first letters of both a girl and her fiancé's birthstones.

Another popular type of ring from the past was the Gemel or Gimmel ring – two, sometimes three bands linked together to form one ring. A favourite design of the nineteenth century was of two bands which when fitted together to form a solid ring enclosed a heart which was held by the third band. At the betrothal ceremony the bands were separated and blessed over a Bible. With a three-link gimmel, the central band that had the heart on it was kept by the witness at the ceremony. When the marriage contract was finally performed at the altar, the pieces were brought together and used as one ring at the ceremony.

The two-part gimmel ring could be worn as separate rings, half each for the man and woman. At the wedding the two parts were fitted together and worn by the bride as one ring, thus symbolizing the essential unity of a married couple.

Martin Luther has often been credited with the introduction of the gimmel ring, and in the early Lutheran period in Germany it became common for the bride and groom to exchange rings. Today in Britain the double-ring ceremony, symbolizing the exchange of vows, is increasingly popular. In some parts of the world it is usual to buy a set of three rings, an engagement ring for the girl and two matching wedding rings for the bride and groom.

The earliest recorded diamond engagement ring was given to Mary of Burgundy in 1477 by her fiancé Archduke Maximilian of Hapsburg. Although until the nineteenth century only royalty and the very rich could afford diamonds, little did he know he would set a trend for so many centuries. Platinum only began to be used for rings at the end of the last century, and gold has been traditionally used as far back in history as we can get. While most people strove to buy a ring, the very poor often had to borrow a ring for the ceremony and hand it back to its owner afterwards. In more recent times until it became so expensive, 22-carat gold, symbolizing the nobility of marriage, was used most for wedding rings and a plain gold band was the most usual type. But in the 1950s new machinery was invented for decorating gold and since then a wide range of fancy, intricate patterns has become available through the method of 'diamond cutting'.

If patterned rings are recent, rings with messages and inscriptions on them are far from modern and have a long history. The Ancient Greeks inscribed Z E Σ meaning 'mayest thou live' and there were Jewish Mizpah rings with the words (taken from Genesis 31, 49) 'The Lord watch between thee and me'. Germans in the sixteenth and seventeenth centuries favoured engravings of Adam and Eve and the tree of temptation, and the Romans liked two hearts held by a key. In Ireland, gold Claddagh rings were decorated with a heart clasped by two hands and given by a mother to the first of her daughters to be married.

The tradition of wearing rings on the left hand has

always continued in Britain, but in parts of Europe they are worn on the right hand. A very old custom in Denmark is of a combined engagement and wedding ring for the bride. When worn on the third finger of the left hand it signifies that the woman is engaged and then on marriage it is changed to the third finger of the right hand. Very often the husband wears a similar combined ring.

Engaged couples in Germany wear plain gold bands on their left hands. The minister who will be marrying the couple takes the rings before the wedding and during the ceremony gives them back to the couple who then place them on the ring finger of their partner's right hand. An ancient Arab custom is the reverse of this – the engagement ring is worn on the right and changed during the marriage ceremony to the left hand.

Incidentally, it was only about a century ago that betrothals became known as engagements. Previously, betrothals had been blessed by the church and were legally binding. Sometimes, if the man should be going on a journey, for instance, a betrothal was celebrated by the breaking of a silver or gold coin, preferably in a jagged way, and the man and woman each kept a piece. This contract, too, was seen as binding. Even today it is still considered unlucky to lose an engagement ring, the loss being seen as a portent of disaster, quarrels or death, and with the ring symbolizing the irreversible nature of marriage, the return of the engagement ring is still considered necessary today if the marriage does not take place.

Romantic human beings that we are, love tokens

and gifts have been exchanged between lovers down the centuries. They are often exchanged to seal a contract further. In Wales, the long winter evenings were often spent carving intricate spoons as love gifts, their long handles decorated with intricate and elaborate designs. Motifs included birds, flowers, initials and dates, key shapes and linked hearts. In lace-making counties bobbins, sometimes made from bones saved from other wedding feasts, were carved, and in areas where knitting was the chief occupation a needle sheath made of bone or wood was a favourite gift. The Irish favoured the harvest knot, the Scots a brooch, and in England there was the 'countryman's favour' – a plaited cornstalk. If the corngrains were left on, it signified the babies that would come during marriage. Handmade gifts of all types were popular love tokens, including wooden cake and butter moulds and spoons, pincushions of a heart shape with the pins arranged in a loving message, decorated china and heart-shaped snuff and trinket boxes.

11

Choosing the Music

Music is an essential part of a church wedding, adding to the beauty of the ceremony. It reflects the mood and development of the service, from the solemn entrance of the bride as she walks up the aisle, through the sacred moments of the taking of vows to the happy procession of the bride and groom, their families and attendants as they leave the church. Taking time to choose the music will add to the enjoyment of the service – for you and your guests.

When seeing the vicar to arrange the date for the wedding, ask for the name and telephone number of the organist at the church. Arrange to see him or her after a Sunday service, choir practice or at a time suitable for all of you, and discuss the music to be played. Organists will be pleased that you have sought them out for advice and are much more likely to practise and play well if they feel wanted and have been consulted! Your minister will be able to guide you through the type of music you may wish to have and will probably have some suggestions of his own – as will the organist. You may find ideas by looking at some Order of Service sheets from previous weddings at the church.

Not every church has an organist with the ability to play to recital standard or deal with pieces as complicated as Widor's Toccata or Bach's Toccata and Fugue in D minor. Nor, in many cases, can church organs! You may have to be realistic and work within the limitations of both organist and organ. When you meet the organist, listen to his or her ideas. You will probably have some of your own but he will know what he can play well and what the organ itself can produce, and will also be knowledgable about music that would be particularly suitable for your chosen style of wedding. He should be able to help you on the subjects of choir and soloists – a talented singer or trumpeter, perhaps.

If you have a friend who is an organist, or if there is no regular organist at the church, it is usually possible to call in someone else, although there may be a ruling that no one other than the official organist may play the organ. The vicar or minister should be able to advise, but as a courtesy you may have to pay a fee to the 'resident' organist if you want someone else to play in his place.

The Bridal Chorus from Wagner's *Lohengrin* ('Here Comes the Bride') was chosen by Princess Louise of Wales at her wedding in 1899, and has been popular ever since. Much *too* popular, many think! There are plenty of alternatives that are enjoyed by brides (and their wedding guests) as music to walk down the aisle to, including Purcell's joyful Trumpet Tune in D, Clarke's Trumpet Voluntary (chosen by Prince Charles because it was 'stirring and dramatic'), Demuth's Processional, Handel's minuet from the 'Music for the Royal Fireworks', and Guilmant's

Wedding March. It's important to get the timing right for the entrance of the bride – don't choose a very long piece of music if the aisle is quite short. The Duchess of York chose Elgar's 'Imperial March' for her wedding entrance in July 1986 – but that was in Westminster Abbey. (She left the Abbey to Elgar's Triumphal March from *Caractacus*, and William Walton's 'Crown Imperial'.) Other pieces of solemn music with dramatic chords, ideal for the entry of the bride, are one of the three fanfares composed for weddings by Arthur Bliss, the hornpipe from Handel's 'Water Music' also Handel's 'Arrival of the Queen of Sheba', Walton's 'Orb and Sceptre', Bach's chorale prelude 'In dir ist Freude' and Peter Hurford's Processional from Laudate Dominum.

Songs or hymns of praise can also be used as processionals for the entry of the bride. Suggestions include 'Praise, my soul, the King of heaven', and 'Glorious things of thee are spoken'. The Queen Mother chose to walk to the altar to 'Lead us, heavenly Father, lead us' and the Duchess of Kent chose Parry's Laudate Dominum for her entrance at York Minster. The advantage of having a hymn, which can be sung by the choir and congregation, is that the length can be tailored by limiting the number of verses to be sung – ideal when the aisle is a short one.

How many hymns are sung, and at which moments in the ceremony, will depend on the minister or vicar, but it is usually three: the first after the entrance of the bride, the second after the Marriage and Benediction, the third after the Prayers and Final Blessing. St Paul's Cathedral rang out to the sound of 'Christ is Made the sure foundation' when the young Lady Diana Spencer stood hand in hand with her Prince at the high altar, and the Duke and Duchess of York chose 'Praise to the Lord, the Almighty, the King of creation' at a similar moment. Later in that service, 'Come down, O Love divine' was sung. Other favourites from royal weddings include 'O perfect Love' (The Duke and Duchess of Windsor chose that), 'Jesu, joy of man's desiring' (Prince Philip and the Queen), 'Glorious things of thee are spoken' (Mark Phillips and Princess Anne) and Gustav Holst's 'I vow to thee my country' (chosen by the Prince and Princess of Wales). Other hymns you might consider for your wedding are 'The King of love my Shepherd is', 'Jerusalem', 'All people that on earth do dwell', 'Now thank we all our God', and 'Love divine, all loves excelling'. There are modern hymns, too, which have become popular choices, such as 'Amazing grace', 'Morning has broken' and 'It's a gift to be simple' (the original hymn to the tune of 'Lord of the Dance'), while some modern songs have also found their way into wedding ceremonies: 'A Whiter Shade of Pale', some of Lennon and McCartney's hits, music from *Jesus Christ Superstar* and the theme from *Chariots of Fire*.

If you have some of your own favourites, then try to include them, but do be sure to read through all the words of hymns or psalms. Some start off well but later lines are of doubtful value at a wedding – for example 'Dear Lord and Father of mankind' has the lines 'Forgive our foolish ways! Re-clothe us in our rightful mind'! It's always preferable to choose hymns and psalms that the congregation is likely to know (and be sure the setting *you* know is the one the organist is used to playing!). Even if a good choir is to sing at your wedding, guests like to sing, or at least join in, with recognized hymns. So do have one or two popular choices that will make everyone feel that they are participating in the service.

There is a good selection of suitable psalms for a wedding: consider psalm 67 (God be merciful unto us, and bless us), psalm 121 (I will lift up mine eyes), psalm 122 (I was glad when they said unto me), psalm 128 (Blessed are all they that fear the Lord) and psalm 150 (O praise God in his holiness). 'The Lord is my shepherd', the hymn version of psalm 23, is often chosen when guests may find a psalm too difficult to sing.

Of the many suitable anthems for a choir to sing, you might choose Walton's 'Set me as a seal upon thine heart' (chosen by the Duke and Duchess of York), 'How lovely are thy dwellings' from Brahms' Requiem, and the Bach/Gounod Ave Maria. An anthem specially commissioned for the wedding of Prince Charles and Lady Diana was 'Let the people praise thee, O God', by William Matthias (but you'll need a good organist and choir to tackle that!). Handel's Largo, Brahms' 'A Rose Has Bloomed', Bach's Air on a G String, Pachelbel's Canon in D, Schubert's Ave Maria, also Adagio in G minor by Albinoni and 'Pièces en style libre' by Vierne are all good pieces of music to play during the signing of the register. The Yorks chose Mozart's Laudate Dominum and Exultate, Jubilate, but whatever you choose for this moment – classical, traditional or modern, played by the organist or sung by a choir or soloist – remember that this music will be played to a silent congregation, waiting for you to return from the vestry. The soloist, and the music, must be enjoyable.

Finally, the triumphal grand finale and wonderful, jubilant music. You could leave the church to Handel's 'Music for the Royal Fireworks', Widor's Toccata from his Symphony No 5 (ever popular, chosen by the Duke and Duchess of Kent when they were married at York Minster in 1961 but not easy to play), Guilmant's 'Grand Choeur' in D, Widor's 'Marche Pontificale', Mulet's 'Carillon Sortie', 'Alla Marcia' by John Ireland, Gigout's 'Grand Choeur Dialogue', the first movement of Mendelssohn's Sonata No 3 in A major, Vierne's 'Carillon de Westminster', Norman Cocker's Tuba Tune, Karg Elert's 'Now thank we all our God' chorale fantasia, Bach's Prelude and Fugue in C – or do as the Princess Royal did when she married Prince Frederick William of Prussia in 1858 . . . she chose the Wedding March from Mendelssohn's *A Midsummer Night's Dream*, and countless millions of brides have done so ever since.

The organist will be playing peaceful music for about a quarter of an hour before the ceremony begins, while the guests are arriving. He is sure to have his own repertoire, but if there are some special pieces of music you'd like him to play, do ask. These might include Handel's Largo, Bach's Air on a G String, Wesley's Air and Gavotte, Elgar's 'Nimrod' and Bach's 'Sheep may safely graze'.

Faced with a list of titles, many of which may be unfamiliar to you, can make choosing the music for your wedding feel like a minefield rather than a pleasure. However, many compilations of music suitable for weddings are now available on records and cassettes, so look on the shelves of record shops and in church bookshops, and check with your local library, for they may have some you could borrow. Listening to a selection at home before you see the organist will give you a much better idea of the type of music you would like to hear at your wedding. If you want something special that the organist doesn't have in his repertoire (and if he or she is prepared to learn it for you) buy the sheet music well ahead of time. You'll also need to check whether any hymns or songs you intend to print in the Order of Service sheet require an acknowledgement or permission to be published.

Incidentally, payment for the organist, choir and soloist, also the bellringers, should be discussed beforehand and the money handed to them, in sealed envelopes, by the best man before the wedding service. And if you are making a sound recording, the organist should be paid one and a half times his normal fee; for a video recording, the usual fee should be doubled.

Do spend time choosing the music, for it can make your special day even more memorable.

12

The Flowers

Flowers are an integral and important part of the wedding day – the bride's bouquet, bridesmaids' posies, buttonholes for the men, corsages for the women, plus flowers to decorate the church or register office and reception.

At the church

While most people enjoy arranging flowers, this is one area of the wedding preparation where brides tend to look with relief to the professionals. However, professional arrangements tend to be expensive, so if a kindly friend or relative with genuine expertise offers to 'do the flowers', accept with alacrity and thanks.

Check first of all with the vicar who may have some very decided views on floral arrangements in his church – where they may or may not be put. Sometimes there are parishioners on the 'flower rota' of the church who will do arrangements in exchange for a donation to church funds. Ask, too, whether there will be any other weddings on the same day. If there are, you could get together with the other brides and see if one lot of flowers will suffice for all the ceremonies on that day, and split the costs between you, so combining ideas, expertise and expense with others.

Having asked and received permission to decorate the church with flowers it is a nice gesture to leave them there for Sunday services. However, the clergyman may wish them to be removed, in which case brides often donate them to a local hospital, children's or old people's home, or send them to a close relative who is unable to be present at the wedding.

The florist doing the bouquet and providing the flowers for decoration may give a discount on whole boxes of flowers; alternatively, especially if you are having a spring or summer wedding, garden flowers can be used and so costs can be cut to a minimum.

Cramming the church with flowers is not necessary. Arrangements in a few strategic points such as around the font and pulpit and either side of the chancel steps will suffice, but think about decorating the porch and placing simple arrangements on windowsills. Consider the size of the church when planning the floral decor – a cathedral would need huge formal arrangements, whereas a village church would look more attractive and cosier if decorated with smaller, more informal bowls. Enquire whether flowers may be placed on the altar.

The font, usually being near the church door, is good to decorate as it will provide a 'welcome' to the guests when they arrive and will be seen as they leave. The pulpit is a striking focal point from all angles of the church, and flowers placed there will be seen from the pews before and during the service.

Arrangements are best kept at eye level, which will probably mean using pedestals. Placed on either side of the altar, they frame the bride and groom, and surprisingly are not too difficult to arrange. A large dish, tightly packed with water-soaked oasis and covered with 5 cm mesh chicken wire, is placed on top of the pedestal. Florist tubes (which can be home-made by attaching green-painted cigar-holders to a cane with sticky tape) are used for holding small and short-stemmed flowers. The tube holders can be kept out of sight by hiding them behind a triangular arrangement of tall sprays of foliage. Start with the small, paler blooms at the top of the arrangement coming down into bigger, more colourful flowers. To avoid a flat impression, recess some flowers. The bulk of the flowers will be at the front, so the back of the arrangement should be weighted to avoid the whole thing toppling over.

As an extra decoration for the church, balls of oasis stuck with small pretty flowers and plenty of greenery can be hung with ribbons from the end of alternate pews, and vases of flowers placed on window sills add an extra splash of colour. Consider having garlands and swags of foliage and flowers. An autumn wedding lends itself particularly well to this type of decoration, for there will be an abundance of seed heads, fruits and berries to be gathered.

The Bride's bouquet

Most brides want a formal bouquet arrangement to carry, and go to the local florist for this. A good florist will have plenty of ideas for designs, using flowers in season. The type of dress you wear and your own height and size will help to indicate the style of bouquet you carry. If you are small, a Victorian-style posy looks more attractive than a huge bouquet. A single flower design based on lilies or orchids is classic and elegant. Pink roses are always popular with brides whatever the time of year. A spring bride could carry tulips, daffodils or a few iris, with hyacinth, freesia or stephanotis, and for a summer wedding, roses and carnations with delphinium or larkspur are beautiful. If you are carrying a prayer book, a spray of flowers like a mini-bouquet is pretty – perhaps freesias, lily of the valley, orchids, sweet peas or stephanotis with a trail of foliage.

Fresh flowers can also be used as a headdress – rosebuds, for example, or lily of the valley, forget-me-nots and pinks intertwined with ivy and made into a coronet. One large brilliant flower slipped into the bride's hair or attached to a veil looks attractive.

Bridesmaids and others

To continue the colour scheme, for the bridesmaids choose flowers that echo the bridal bouquet or prayer book spray. The groom can wear a buttonhole of one of the types of flowers contained in the bride's bouquet. A little basket of flowers, light and easy to hold, looks charming when carried by a small child and a pomander or flower ball can be made to suit the tiniest flower girl or made larger for an adult bridesmaid. The colours of the flowers should complement their gowns. Corsages for the important guests, including both mothers, should follow the colour scheme of the wedding flowers and blend well with their outfits.

At the register office

Register offices can be a bit bare, though some are beautifully decked out with flowers. Check on floral arrangements with the registrar when you see him to book the date of the wedding. If it is unlikely that the room will be decorated with flowers, delegate a friend or relative to take a pretty floral arrangement with them into the room for the ceremony. They can be taken away again afterwards and used at the reception.

Silk flowers

Silk flowers are becoming more and more popular for bridal bouquets for a variety of reasons. Mainly, of course, because they can be kept for a very long time, and many brides like to make them into table decorations for the new home. Silk flowers are now looking so much more professional and 'real'-looking. Their main advantage is that they can be colour- and shade-matched to the wedding dress and bridesmaids' dresses with much greater accuracy than fresh flowers, and as there is no growing season any bloom can be available at any time of the year.

For the reception

Flowers and foliage brighten up a buffet reception in a local hall. Some simple arrangements on the table – pink and white carnations or posies of spring flowers such as primroses – look pretty and are easy to do. Keep them low so they don't obscure faces across the table. Cream or yogurt pots can be painted white, silver or gold, with oasis placed in the bottom of each. Spring flowers and sprays of flowers such as spray carnations, miniature roses and spray chrysanthemums look particularly pretty, though any garden flowers will do. Guests can take them away as souvenirs. Or copy a Romanian custom of a trail of fresh blooms laid down the centre of long tables.

Posies can be placed at regular intervals on long tables with a few more around the bride and groom. With the cake as a central focal point at the reception, asymmetrical arrangements can be used on either side. A pedestal display behind the bride and groom makes a good backdrop for photographs, especially for the cutting of the cake. But in general, large, costly and formal arrangements are lost at a reception, whereas delicate posy bowls will be emphasized and remembered. It is traditional for a silver vase holding a few flowers to be set on top of the cake, preferably containing some blooms to match the bride's bouquet. Small flowers can be placed around the base of the cake, too.

Colours for the reception flowers are a matter of preference, but brides often like to continue the colour scheme chosen for the church, carrying it through to the reception tables. It is a nice touch to pick out shades from the bridesmaids' dresses.

One way to make a few flowers go a long way is to use plenty of foliage. Green leaves give coolness and freshness, soft grey leaves combine well with rose-coloured flowers, and a few trailing tendrils give an informality and softness to an arrangement.

A trail of honeysuckle, a branch of blossom, pussy willow and daffodils, a crowd of bluebells, primroses or michaelmas daisies – or in the winter, holly, ivy, winter-flowering shrubs and Christmas roses – make a wedding seasonal and very personal. Nature's colours always blend beautifully, so you need never be afraid to mix flowers – remember the country cottage garden full of life and colour.

For a reception held in a marquee, the floral decorations will need to be high or they will get lost in the crowd. Ropes of foliage wired on to rolls of newspaper can be twisted around the poles and a few flowers inserted just before the guests arrive. Baskets of flowers can be hung at eye level and ribbon bows can also be used for splashes of colour either instead of flowers (to avoid wilting), or mixed with them.

Receptions held at home can make use of any of the above ideas, though scaled down. Little pot trees are easy to make and look effective. Put a piece of cane about 25 cm long into a small flower pot. Weight the pot with stones and fix the cane firmly in place with plaster mixture. Wrap a ball of oasis in silver foil, attach it to the top of the cane, and stick in tiny flowers and green leaves. Tie a matching ribbon underneath to prevent the ball from slipping. Both the cane and the pot can be painted to match the bride's colour scheme. Pedestals can be hired – and consider hiring a host of pot plants, too, for decoration. Don't forget the front door – a garland hung there makes a beautiful welcome to your home – and fireplaces and banisters seem to invite floral decorations.

At a hotel or restaurant, flowers for the reception may be part of the package. Do check that their colours will harmonize with your colour scheme, and ask if the hotel will allow extra floral decoration to be put in on the day by a member of your wedding party. One huge display placed at the entrance to the room will be enjoyed by guests waiting in the receiving line.

Flowers in season

Many flowers that are out of season here are flown in from countries around the world, which should ensure that the flowers you want will be available when you want them. However, when special orders are taken for a specific colour bloom of a species out of season in our own country, there is always the possibility that the order cannot be made up exactly when required. By ordering flowers in season you have a much better chance of them being available, and they will also be less expensive.

The following is a list of flowers ideal for weddings, the time of year when they are available and when they are 'best buys'.

JANUARY
Available – carnations, chrysanthemums, tulips, freesias, irises, violets, anemones, lilies, lilies of the valley.
Best buys – narcissus, daffodils.

FEBRUARY
Available – all year round chrysanthemums, irises, violets, anemones, lilies of the valley, lilies, roses, carnations.
Best buys – narcissus, daffodils, tulips, freesias.

MARCH
Available – all year round chrysanthemums, lilies of the valley, lilies, sweet peas, stocks, roses, carnations.
Best buys – narcissus, daffodils, tulips, freesias, irises, violets, anemones.

APRIL
Available – gladioli.
Best buys – narcissus, daffodils, all year round chrysanthemums, tulips, freesias, irises, violets, anemones, lilies of the valley, lilies, sweet peas, stocks, roses, carnations.

MAY
Available – narcissus, daffodils, freesias, gladioli, chrysanthemums.
Best buys – all year round chrysanthemums, tulips, irises, violets, anemones, lilies of the valley, lilies, sweet peas, stocks, roses, carnations.

JUNE
Available – tulips, gladioli, chrysanthemums.
Best buys – all year round chrysanthemums, irises,
violets, lilies of the valley, lilies, sweet peas, stocks,
roses, carnations.

JULY
Available – lilies of the valley.
Best buys – all year round chrysanthemums, irises,
lilies, sweet peas, stocks, roses, carnations,
gladioli, dahlias, asters, chrysanthemums.

AUGUST
Available – all year round chrysanthemums, lilies of
the valley, lilies, stocks.
Best buys – roses, carnations, gladioli, dahlias, asters,
chrysanthemums.

SEPTEMBER
Available – all year round chrysanthemums, freesias,
irises, violets, lilies of the valley, stocks.
Best buys – roses, carnations, gladioli, dahlias, asters,
chrysanthemums.

OCTOBER
Available – all year round chrysanthemums, freesias,
irises, violets, lilies of the valley, lilies, stocks,
gladioli.
Best buys – anemones, roses, carnations, dahlias,
asters, chrysanthemums.

NOVEMBER
Available – all year round chrysanthemums, freesias,
irises, anemones, lilies of the valley, lilies, roses,
carnations.
Best buys – chrysanthemums.

DECEMBER
Available – narcissus, daffodils, all year round
chrysanthemums, freesias, irises, violets,
anemones, lilies of the valley, lilies, roses,
carnations.
Best buys – chrysanthemums.

Flowers of the zodiac

Aquarius (Jan 20 – Feb 18) daffodils
Pisces (Feb 19 – Mar 20) freesias
Aries (March 21 – April 20) tulips
Taurus (April 21 – May 20) iris
Gemini (May 21 – June 20) stocks
Cancer (June 21 – July 21) roses
Leo (July 22 – Aug 21) carnations
Virgo (Aug 22 – Sept 22) gladioli
Libra (Sept 23 – Oct 22) dahlias
Scorpio (Oct 23 – Nov 21) chrysanthemums
Sagittarius (Nov 22 – Dec 20) anemones
Capricorn (Dec 21 – Jan 19) narcissus

Flowers and their meanings

Folklore has it that special meanings are attached to
flowers. Romantics might like to make up a bouquet
with a message!

lily – majesty
forget-me-not – true love
lily of the valley –
  happiness
orange blossom –
  fertility
snowdrop – hope
carnation – deep love
narcissus – egotism

honeysuckle – fidelity
cornflower – hope
rose – love
hyacinth – constancy
sweet pea – pleasure
violet – faithfulness
camellia – gratefulness
larkspur – fickleness
buttercup – riches

Roses may be dedicated to the goddesses of love, but the colours are relevant too – a red rose means 'I love you', white symbolizes virginity, rosebuds indicate young and innocent love, and a yellow rose is supposed to signify jealousy and infidelity! Red tulips declare love, white chrysanthemums truth, while lilies purity. Herbs have their place and meanings, too: sage for riches or health, rosemary for remembrance, mint for virtue and parsley for festivity.

Planning and preparation

Preparation for all the floral displays should begin about two days before the wedding, but the planning and ordering ahead should be done some time beforehand. Freshness is all important in any arrangement, as is the planning of a colour scheme, blending in first of all with what the bride wants and linking it to the bridesmaids' dresses and dominant colours in the church, register office or reception.

When ordering the flowers, encourage the interest of the florist and get her advice on the life expectancy of flowers you particularly like and whether they would be suitable for the use you want to make of them. Anything likely to fade and wilt before the wedding day is over should be carefully avoided, however pretty. Order the flowers well in advance, making sure to ask for a few more than you think will be absolutely necessary. Arrange for their delivery or collection in good time. Neither flowers nor their arrangers respond well to last-minute panic.

When the flowers arrive, follow the instructions given by the florist to keep them in peak condition. Most advise that the stems of roses should be cut on a slant to expose a wider 'drinking area' and remove the natural seal produced to preserve moisture while out of water. For safety and ease of arrangement, it is a good idea to remove any thorns. Spray carnations, it is often suggested, should have about 2½ cm cut from the stem and the foliage stripped to about halfway up.

All flowers should be plunged to the neck in water (not icy cold) as soon as possible. Soak all the greenery for arrangements in the bath, completely submerged, so it will stand up well and not wilt.

The big displays can be done on the day before the wedding and topped up with water in the morning, removing anything that is flagging or wilting. The smaller displays, such as those for the pulpit, lectern, font, window sill and for the reception tables should be done on the day if there is enough time before the ceremony.

Seeing the florist

Most good florists will have a design guide from which the bride can choose the shape and style of bouquet she would like to have. They will also be able to give advice on the type to choose, bearing in mind a combination of flowers, colours and shapes that will suit the wedding dress style and material. So, if the dress is being specially made, take along a piece of the material and picture of the pattern. Similarly, if flowers are to be worn in the hair, the florist would want to see any headdress or veil that was going to be worn. When it is not a large bouquet that is needed but simply a spray or corsage for pinning to a dress, jacket, handbag or hat, the florist would want to see the outfit that is going to be worn so a spray of flowers can be designed to match.

The florist will also blend the bridesmaids' bouquets to match the bride's flowers. Like those for the bride, the attendants' flowers should always be chosen to complement the colour and style of dress. It is traditional for bridesmaids to carry a posy, but flower baskets, pomanders or flower balls are also very popular. The florist will need to know the approximate ages and sizes of the attendants – for a small flower girl would not need the same size bouquet as would an adult bridesmaid – and will also want to know if something special like a flower parasol or special headdress is required for any of the attendants.

If the florist is being asked to do all the flowers for the wedding, he or she may suggest carrying the chosen theme and colours of the bride's bouquet and the flowers of the attendants through to the church and reception. They may suggest a visit to the church with the bride and her mother to discuss flower arrangements, and also design table arrangements for the reception and a spray to decorate the top of the wedding cake.

The florist will also suggest suitable flowers for buttonholes and corsages to suit everyone specially concerned with the wedding. With dress rules more relaxed now, special buttonholes are often made up for the groom that match the colour of his suit, shirt or tie, and the overall effect is very attractive if the flower chosen is also represented in the bride's bouquet.

Memories of the flowers at your wedding can last for a very long time – some can be pressed or dried, or petals pressed and made into a collage and framed. There are people who do this as a hobby or professionally. Look for small ads in magazines or ask at local craft fairs.

13

The Photographer

Choose a professional photographer who has been recommended, if possible, and who specializes in wedding photography. If you do not know one, visit some studios and shops in your area and ask to see samples of their recent work. Discuss the type of photographs you want, get a quotation and be sure you know precisely what the quotation includes.

You will want an album and set of prints for yourselves; some couples like to order two more complete albums to give to their parents as presents.

A good professional photographer will manage to get groups of people together and make them feel and look relaxed. The best group pictures are ones where people are smiling or talking to each other or at least not all staring straight into the camera lens.

With video recorders now in widespread use and readily available for hire, you may decide to have a videotape made of your wedding. Contact the local specialists in this and try to talk to other couples who have used them. Charges vary, so always get quotations. If possible, arrange for the videotape to be played back during the reception for everyone there to see.

Too many formal photographs on the wedding day

can be time-consuming and tiresome. Some couples like to go to a nearby park or garden specifically for formal photographs to be taken after the wedding and before the reception and then have plenty of informal shots taken during the day and the celebrations. Arrange to have a good mixture of formal and informal pictures, both to appease family members and for your own enjoyment in the future. Here are some ideas for photographs you are likely to want to have taken:

Before the ceremony

Bride getting dressed in gown; mother adjusting headdress and veil; chief bridesmaid arranging the veil; bride with father leaving the house for the ceremony; bride with both parents; bride with brides-maids; groom and best man leaving for church; groom and ushers adjusting buttonholes; bride with father at and in the car; bride stepping into/out of the car; bride arriving with father at the church; bride and groom's families arriving at the church.

At the ceremony (if photography is allowed – never use flash)

Parents and guests being seated by ushers; interior of the church; altar and flowers; organist, choir or musicians; the processional up the aisle; exchange of vows and rings; bride and groom signing the register; witnesses signing the register; recessional from the church.

After the ceremony

Bride and groom outside the church; entire wedding party grouped outside the church; bride and groom with the bridesmaids; bridesmaids with the best man and ushers; bride and groom leaving for the reception; bride and groom in the car; bride and groom with the bride's parents and with the groom's parents.

At the reception

Bride and groom together; the receiving line – before and while receiving guests; the top table; tables with food; bride and groom cutting the cake; close-up of their joined hands on the cake knife; at the toasts and speeches; on the dance floor; bride and groom chatting to guests; family at the wedding party; small informal groups of guests chatting; bride tossing her bouquet; girl who caught the bouquet; groom removing bride's garter; groom throwing garter and man catching it; the couple leaving the reception; the bride and groom in the going-away car; guests throwing confetti; close-up of decorations on bridal car.

14

Wedding Invitations

Once the wedding date, type of reception and venue have been decided upon and the bride's mother (after discussion with the bridegroom's family) has drawn up a guest list, the invitation cards can be ordered and sent out. Post them at least four weeks but preferably six weeks before the wedding date. They should be ordered well in advance to allow for printing.

For a small wedding the invitations can be hand-written; otherwise you should visit a stationer and place your order for printed cards after looking at the samples of types and designs available. Paper, size, type face (style of lettering) and wording will have to be chosen. Lettering should be simple and easy to read – black is the traditional choice. Special insertions can be ordered at the same time including reply cards and envelopes, hotel reservation cards for out-of-town guests, reception invitations and maps. Some people choose a four-sided invitation that includes a map on the back page. Ask the stationer for a 'guarantee of replacement'. This will ensure that if a mistake is made in the printing the cards will be replaced free of charge.

While a reply card is not essential and does add to

the cost (possibly including higher postage if a fairly heavy paper has been chosen), it does make organizing much easier. People are much more likely to respond quickly if all they have to do is to post back a ready printed card. It also makes it easier to keep track of replies and acceptances. Include a stamped self-addressed envelope with the reply card.

Other extras to be ordered from the stationer may include serviettes, matchbooks, cake boxes and order of service sheets.

If all the invitations are to be sent to people who will be attending both the ceremony and the reception, the information on both venues can be included on the invitation card. However, if some guests are only to be invited to the ceremony or only to the reception, separate cards will be required. If the church or register office is small it may only be possible to invite a small number of people to be present at the ceremony, but many more may be invited to celebrate at the reception or an evening disco.

It may be decided (although it's not customary) to have a large number of friends and family at the ceremony, but only to invite a few people to a sit-down restaurant meal afterwards. Whatever the situation, it should be made clear within the wording of the invitation exactly what the guests are being invited to. Invitations generally come from the bride's parents, indicating that they are paying for the reception.

The wording of the invitation card depends on who is the host and/or hostess and their relationship to the bride. There are two ways for including the names of the guests, either handwritten in the top left-hand corner or on a line provided within the wording of the invitation. The latter style is generally the most popular and this has been used in the following examples of wording.

Where both parents of the bride are the host and hostess, the invitation would read:

Mr and Mrs James Green
request the pleasure of
the company of

_____

at the marriage of their
daughter
Victoria
to
Mr John Smith
at St Saviour's Church
Welbridge
on Saturday, 2nd May
at 3 o'clock
and afterwards at
The County Hotel, Welbridge.

RSVP

18 Honeycombe Road
Welbridge
Wessex

Where the bride's mother is widowed and is the only hostess:

Mrs James Green
requests the pleasure of
the company of

_____

at the marriage
of her daughter
Victoria
to
Mr John Smith etc.

Where the bride's father is the only host, the wording is:

Mr James Green
requests the pleasure of
the company of

_____

at the marriage
of his daughter
Victoria etc.

Where the bride's mother has remarried and she and the bride's stepfather are the host and hostess:

Mr and Mrs Luke Williams
request the pleasure of the
company of

_____

at the marriage of her
daughter
Victoria etc.

In this case the bride's surname may be included if she has not adopted her stepfather's name, eg.

> Mr and Mrs Luke Williams
> request the pleasure of the
> company of

> _____

> at the marriage of her
> daughter
> Victoria Green
> to, etc.

Where the bride's father and stepmother are the host and hostess:

> Mr and Mrs James Green
> request the pleasure of
> the company of

> _____

> at the marriage of
> his daughter
> Victoria
> to, etc.

Where the bride's stepmother is the hostess:

> Mrs James Green
> requests the pleasure of
> the company of

> _____

> at the marriage of her
> stepdaughter
> Victoria
> to, etc.

If the bride's parents are divorced, they may still be the joint host and hostess and the wording on the invitation should read:

> Mr James Green
> and
> Mrs Jane Green
> request the pleasure of
> the company of
>
> _____
>
> at the marriage of their
> daughter
> Victoria to, etc.

If either of the bride's parents have remarried, then the subsequent husband or wife does not play a prominent part at the wedding. In the case of the bride's mother remarrying but being joint hostess with the bride's father the invitation would read:

> Mr James Green
> and
> Mrs George Thomas
> request the pleasure of
> the company of
>
> _____
>
> at the marriage of their
> daughter
> Victoria, etc.

If the bride's relatives, other than mother and father, are the host and hostess the invitation should read:

Mr and Mrs Arthur Brown
request the pleasure of
the company of

_____

at the marriage of their
niece/ward/his(her)
goddaughter
Victoria, etc.

The bride's surname may be added if different from the host's and hostess's.

If relatives of the bride who are not husband and wife are the host and hostess (eg. brother and sister, brother and sister-in-law, or sisters) invitations should be worded:

– in the case of brother and sister:

Mr John Brown
and
Miss Jane Brown
request the pleasure . . .

– when the sister is married:

Mr John Brown
and
Mrs Arthur Green
request the pleasure of . . .

– brother and sister-in-law:

Mr John Brown and
Mrs George Brown
request the pleasure . . .

– unmarried sisters:

> The Misses Brown
> request the pleasure . . .

– where one sister is married:

> Miss Jane Brown and
> Mrs David Williams
> request the pleasure . . .

– at a double wedding, if the brides are sisters, the invitation is issued jointly:

> Mr and Mrs James Green
> request the pleasure of the
> company of

_____

> at the marriage of their daughters
> Victoria
> to Mr John Smith
> and
> Helen
> to Mr Martin Brown . . .

If the double wedding is of a sister and brother:

> Mr and Mrs James Green
> and Mr and Mrs Lionel Black
> request the pleasure of the
> company of

_____

> at the marriage of their daughters
> Victoria
> to Mr John Smith
> and
> Susan

to
Mr Matthew Green . . .

If you put both the name and address of the person
to whom the reply should be sent, it avoids confusion
and makes it clear who is the chief organizer of the
wedding.

When the bride and groom are giving the reception
the invitations should read:

> John Smith and Victoria Green
> request the pleasure of the
> company of
>
> _____
>
> at their marriage . . .

or alternatively

> The pleasure of the company
> of
>
> _____
>
> is requested at the marriage of
> Miss Victoria Green
> and
> Mr John Smith . . .

When both sets of parents are jointly giving the
reception, the invitations should read:

> Mr and Mrs James Green
> and Mr and Mrs Peter Smith
> request the pleasure of the
> company of
>
> _____

at the marriage of
Victoria
to
Mr John Smith

The layout of the invitations may vary slightly because although the wording is standard, the design (i.e. how many words on each line and how many lines) does vary and is also dependent on other factors, such as card size.

The wording of invitations to a second marriage is usually less formal than for the first wedding. If the bride's parents are giving a reception they can send out 'At Home' cards reading 'For Jennifer and James'. If the couple are hosts the cards can read 'Jennifer Smith and James Brown have much pleasure in inviting you to a reception at . . . following their wedding . . .', or an informal handwritten letter can be sent to close friends for a small wedding party saying 'Jennifer and James hope you'll join them to celebrate their wedding . . .'

If the wedding has to be cancelled or postponed (after the invitations have been sent out) due to illness, death or a broken engagement, cards should be sent out with the following wording:

– indefinite postponement:

Owing to the recent death of Mr James Smith, Mr and Mrs David Green deeply regret that they are obliged to cancel the invitations to the marriage of their daughter, Victoria, to Mr John Smith at . . . etc.

When a later date is fixed, new invitations should be sent out.

– postponement to a later date:

Owing to the illness of Mrs James Smith, Mr and Mrs David Green deeply regret that they are obliged to postpone the invitations to the marriage of their daughter Victoria to Mr John Smith at St Margaret's Church, Westminster from (date) to (date).

– cancellation because the wedding is to take place quietly:

Owing to the recent death of her husband, Mrs David Green much regrets that she is obliged to cancel the invitation to the marriage of her daughter Victoria to Mr John Smith, which will now take place quietly on . . .

Invitations to the quiet wedding are then sent out by letter to near relations and close friends only.

– cancellation of the wedding – broken engagement:

Mr and Mrs David Green announce that the marriage of their daughter, Victoria, to Mr John Smith, which was arranged for 10th November, will not now take place.

If only a few of the wedding guests are to be invited to the reception the details of the ceremony only will be given on the invitation cards and the invitation to the reception can be handwritten on the bottom of the card, in the third person and without a signature.

A reception-only printed card would read:

Mr and Mrs James Green
request the pleasure of

the company of
_____

at the reception to follow the marriage of their daughter
Victoria to Mr John Smith at the
County Hotel,
Welbridge,
on Saturday, 2nd May, at 4 o'clock
RSVP

If wished, a separate note may be enclosed with
the invitation stating the reason: 'Owing to the small
size of St Saviour's Church it is only possible to ask
a few guests to the service. We hope you will forgive
this invitation being to the reception only.'

If a Service of Blessing is held, the invitation could
read:

Mr and Mrs James Green
request the pleasure of
the company of
_____

at a Service of Blessing
the marriage of
their daughter Victoria . . .

When replying to a wedding invitation (and a reply
card has not been enclosed) the following formal
wording can be used. Replies should be brief, sent
early and written in the third person: 'Mr and Mrs
Richard Carter and their daughter Margaret thank
Mr and Mrs James Green for their kind invitation
to their daughter's wedding at St Saviour's Church,
Welbridge on Saturday, 2nd May at 3 o'clock and to a
reception afterwards at the County Hotel, Welbridge,

and are most happy to accept.' Such a response requires only the address of the sender and the date of the letter. No signature is necessary.

If the invitation cannot be accepted because of a prior engagement or for some private family reason it is polite to decline the invitation as soon as possible. Formal wording for this type of response could be similar to the above, but the last lines instead of reading 'and are most happy to accept' should read 'unfortunately they have accepted a prior engagement for that date and must therefore decline with regret'.

Sometimes an invitation is already accepted but must be declined through last minute illness, accident, or sudden death in the family. In such cases the bride's parents must be notified at once. A simple note is all that is necessary. Again no signature is required and the letter should be dated: 'Mr and Mrs Richard Carter and their daughter Jane sincerely regret the necessity, because of a bereavement in the family, to have to inform you that they will not be able to attend your daughter's wedding on 2nd May, or at a reception afterwards.'

The examples given above are all in formal wording and when a formal wedding is taking place most families wish to conform to this traditional wording of invitations. However, it is no longer essential. A major break from tradition is when the bride and groom themselves are the hosts at their wedding and when they write personal notes to guests on the lines of 'John and I are getting married and we'd love you to be there', giving details of the date, time and place of the ceremony and the reception party or disco afterwards.

15

Choosing a Wedding Dress

How she looks on her wedding day is obviously of great importance to every bride. It is the subject of much discussion and searching for exactly the right dress. Buying a bridal magazine regularly is a useful guide to the latest styles of wedding dresses available in the shops and a clue to price ranges, but there will probably still be plenty of window shopping to be done before the right dress is finally chosen. Look at wedding photographs in newspapers and local photographers' windows, too.

There is a wide variety of styles to choose from, from a simple, elegant silk dress to the 'traditional' style of lace and frills, with or without a train. An all-white dress could be chosen, or white with a colour trim or embroidery, or else one of the warmer shades like cream or peach. A winter wedding suggests long sleeves, heavy dupion silk, light wool challis or similar warmer material. A train might not be advisable in wintry, maybe muddy, conditions.

It is well worth doing plenty of window shopping, visiting bridal shops or the bridal department in big stores, looking at patterns and designs in books and magazines, and trying on a variety of dress styles before making the decision to go on a shopping expedition to buy your wedding dress. If you have a good idea of what you want, as well as what you want to spend, the salesperson can be much more helpful.

When shopping seriously for the dress, if possible avoid the really busy times like Saturdays, when the shop is crowded, space is very limited and it is difficult to get very much personal attention. Take someone along with you whose judgement you value – your mother perhaps, the chief bridesmaid or a close friend. Never drag an army of people or small children along to the shop – they take up a lot of space and you could end up feeling rushed, pressured or hassled.

When planning to try on dresses be prepared and give yourself time to make a choice. Wear (or take with you) shoes with the heel height you plan to be wearing for the wedding and wear a good fitting bra and underwear in white. Go into the shop looking and feeling good. If you are rushed or your hair wants washing and you feel a bit of a mess generally you will not be in an ideal mood to make an important decision or even enjoy choosing your wedding dress. Make this shopping expedition an occasion to enjoy and remember.

If you know a particular style suits you, adapt that line for your wedding dress. A favourite blouse may suggest a suitable neckline – high-collared, sweetheart, cross-over or V-neck, for example; similarly the sleeves – full, slim, puffed or tight fitting. Do you want a full-length dress or would you feel more comfortable with an ankle-length, mid-calf or below-the-knee length? Do you have pretty shoulders or a tiny waist? – then pick a style that shows them off to their best advantage.

Certain styles suit particular figure types. If you are short-waisted pick a dress without a defined waistline – a style that falls freely from bodice to hem will avoid a cut-in-half look. A high neckline and elongated seaming also help. Trying to hide a large bust by flattening it is not a successful ploy, but choosing a dress that does not have a fussy or frilly neck and bustline is. A curving waistline plus simple, slightly flowing (not tight) sleeves are also helpful. Large hips need a loosely cut design without a definite wasitline; the long sweep from top to hem helps minimize a pear-shaped torso. Plump ladies need to cut down on fussy trimmings and to wear high-waisted lines that flow over hips and wide bulges. Tall, slim girls can avoid the beanpole look by choosing a dress with strong horizontal lines, full, flowing sleeves and lace-edged overskirt. A full skirt helps to counter-balance broad shoulders.

These are general hints about design that help to hide or at least minimize figure problems. Few people have perfect figures and as the bride will be the centre of attention she will want to look her very best from every angle. In general, the simpler the style the easier it is to wear and the more elegant it looks. Attention to detail is important. For example, the back of the dress is easy to overlook – but remember that for most of the wedding service this is the view that everyone in the congregation will have of the bride. If you want a train, consider the length of the aisle in the church.

Once the dress has been chosen, there may be

some alterations to be made. Many boutiques keep only sample dresses on the rails and then order or make up a new dress specially for the bride. So always leave plenty of time before the wedding date for alterations and fittings – but not *too* long in case you gain or lose a lot of weight in the intervening months.

When going to the shop for further fittings, always wear the type of bra and underwear that you plan to wear at the wedding, and take along the shoes to be worn. Shoes should be of comfortable heel height – and not worn for the very first time on your wedding day. Check that tights or stockings are the right shade – very pale or white, or colour-co-ordinated with the dress. Choose a bra that makes the most of your figure, suits the neckline of the dress, is not likely to peep out at the neckline if you move, and will not run the risk of having a strap slipping. A dress with a close-fitting bodice requires a plain seamless bra underneath it to avoid an ugly outline. Wearing the right bra to the fitting will ensure that any bust darts are in exactly the right position.

With the dress chosen, you can search for a veil and headdress or a hat and accessories to suit. Ideally, these should be chosen and bought from the same shop so you can look in a mirror and see the outfit together as a whole picture. Veils range from the short to the very long, some are plain net and have a small trim, others have a pattern in the net or a more definite edging. Choose a headdress at the same time to ensure that everything looks right together. Headdresses range from the simple to the elaborate and are usually of entwined white flowers and leaves in a circlet or band that sits across the top of the head. Depending on the style of dress chosen a hat could be worn as an alternative to a headdress and veil, as can a single fresh flower or a handmade headdress of flowers and ribbons.

It is a good idea to look at styles of bridesmaids' dresses, too, and gain some idea of how you want your attendants to look. Will you choose a plain colour or patterned dress and will the smaller bridesmaids wear the same style and colourings as the adults? Will the bridesmaids' dresses be bought from a shop, or handmade at home, or by a dressmaker?

If you are planning to have your bridal dress made rather than buying it from a shop, it is still just as important to do plenty of searching and window shopping for suitable styles, as well as looking at pattern books. If you have set your heart on a one-off designer dress, look in the big stores, go to fashion shows and look at fashion magazines to see the work of the top designers. Then make an appointment with the designer of your choice to discuss the dress that will be designed and created especially for you.

For those brides who do not want to wear a traditional white wedding dress but would like a long dress that could probably be worn again for a special occasion, the evening dress department in the big stores is a good place to look to find something suitable. Small dress shops and boutiques are also often good, both for this type of dress and for a well cut and elegant suit or dress and jacket.

With the dress chosen, fitting to perfection, and brought lovingly home – hang it carefully somewhere

safe, preferably where it can be loosely covered and
not disturbed. Many bridal boutiques offer a service
to give the dress a final press on the day before the
wedding. Practise walking in the dress, especially if
it has a long train. A skirt that is just a fraction too
long can cause a lot of problems, and if you discover
this before the wedding it can be remedied in good
time.

Practise, too, with the veil if you are wearing one.
While you will need to walk gracefully, every movement could affect the security of the veil (as of course
can the weather!). Keep it secure by using several
very fine hairpins or white grips woven into the veil
and through your hair. The headdress can also be
made more secure with some suitably placed double-
sided tape! The flowers and leaves of the headdress
ensure that the tape can be hidden from view.

When planning your hairstyle for the wedding,
always take the headdress with you to the hairdresser so he or she can create a style that not only
suits you but is also suitable for holding the headdress of your choice.

Colour scheming

With so many individuals involved in a wedding
party it is all too easy for everyone individually to
decide on their dress and when everyone gets
together they may all clash terribly. Co-ordinated
colour looks more attractive on the day as well as
being much better for the wedding photographs
which will be kept and looked at over the years.

Once the bride has decided on her colour scheme

– both for herself and the bridesmaids – it is a good idea for the respective mothers (and fathers) to get together to plan their outfits. This prevents mums wearing clashing colours or the same outfits, and ensures that the menfolk will wear suits that blend into the overall scheme.

As an example, the bride may wear white or cream with the bridesmaids in pale lemon. The bride's mother could wear a gold suit with toning hat and shoes and the groom's father would complement her in a stone-coloured suit. The groom could wear grey or brown with the best man in a suit of a darker or lighter shade of the same colour. Granny could wear a prettily patterned brown and cream suit and dress with grandpa in a brown suit. In this 'autumny' colour scheme everyone will look different while making a very attractive overall picture.

The problem of what the men are to wear is removed if it is a formal wedding and dress suits are hired (preferably from the same place). Traditionally, if the groom is wearing formal attire, so too should the fathers of the bride and groom.

The colour scheming can be extended as far as you wish – to the flowers, the decoration of the reception hall and the colour of the icing on the cake.

16

Wedding Day Beauty

Nature is a girl's best friend on her wedding day. That extra bright-eyed sparkle and blush of excitement which comes from inner happiness shines through so strongly that she'll probably never look quite as radiant again! Every bride has a very special natural beauty, but even so there's no harm in helping the beauty process along a little and emphasizing it with good health and pretty make-up. With all eyes and cameras on the bride, it's the day you must look your best among all the excitement, friends, family and photographers.

Some beauty groundwork in the preceding weeks will be repaid with a flawless skin and shining hair. Diet, exercise and skincare are all important – eat lots of green vegetables, salads and fresh fruit, cut down on fats and add extra vitamins to your food intake. For a slimmer, more lithe body, do some exercises, walk more and if possible enrol in a health and beauty club or keep-fit group.

Carry out your cleansing and moisturizing routine meticulously night and day. The odd spot that appears around period time can usually be controlled and covered with a dab of medicated make-up stick or cream and by cutting down on sweet things like chocolate. More serious skin problems need a concentrated effort at clearing them up.

Treat your hair to a good shampoo and conditioner as well as some expert cutting so it is really in tip-top condition for the wedding and honeymoon.

You may like to have a splurge on a more expensive brand of make-up, to feel a little more luxurious on your wedding day. Whatever you decide, think well ahead. Do the rounds of the beauty counters, ask questions, get advice from the make-up specialists in big stores or your local beauty salon. Try out as much as you can with testers. There are often special offers on trial-sized products and these can be great for experimenting at low cost. If you sometimes react to make-up try a hypo-allergenic range.

Your hands will be on show a great deal, especially when you show off your ring and cut the cake. In the weeks leading up to the wedding use hand cream at least twice a day and preferably after every time your hands have been in water. Take time to give yourself a weekly manicure and become nail-conscious. Massage around the nails with cuticle cream and treat soft nails with nail hardener. Give nail polish a rest for a while if you can. The day before the wedding, when nails should be stronger and looking good, having responded to all the extra attention and care, give yourself a manicure. File nails with an emery board, in one direction only, then finalize the manicure on your wedding morning. Apply a base coat, two coats of nail enamel in a pale colour and top coat. Remember that dark, strong or unusual colours will look too hard against a white dress.

Your special day make-up should be strong enough to define your face for photographers but not so strong as to be overpowering. Keep it light and remain recognizably your natural self. Try out every single item you intend to use, well in advance, and practise the look you intend to wear. Put extra thought into it – for example, white can drain colour from skin tones – and bear in mind that you will be seen by lots of people, close up and at a distance, and you'll also be photographed, so a little extra definition on eyes, lips and cheekbones is needed.

Take time to put on a really good foundation. The one you choose should be light and a similar shade to your natural skin tone. Bear in mind that you are likely to be a little flushed with excitement and nerves, so avoid a foundation with too much pink in it. Similarly, avoid suntan shades if you haven't got a tan. Apply it carefully, blending in well.

When choosing a blusher, steer clear of browns and dark reds – go for apricot, soft pink or peach. Dust over lightly with a translucent powder to set foundation and cream blusher. If you prefer a powder blusher, apply this over the translucent powder. A blusher is essential, for it gives colour and life to cheeks and makes eyes look sparkly. A touch used over the browbone warms and lifts your face and makes you look even more radiant. It is better to give your face warmth and colour with blusher than to use a pinky foundation.

Eyes need to be defined, but don't overdo the colours. When applying your base don't neglect your eyelids, as a thin film of foundation makes eyeshadows go on more smoothly and last longer.

Choose eyeshadow colours carefully and practise your eye make-up well before the wedding so you have time to create, and get used to, the look you desire. Powder shadows are usually easier to use. Look for sheer, slightly sheeny shadows with a touch of iridescence. Don't worry about matching your eye colour – just because you have blue eyes it doesn't mean you have to wear blue eye shadow. Pearly browns, shades of amethyst and champagne are all very warm and flattering. Practise blending the shadow shades on your eye and defining the bottom of the eye with a fine pencil or brush.

Mascara must be waterproof! Choose brown or navy, both are softer colours than black, which anyway can close up the eyes rather than make them look larger. A fine pencil or brush line of powder shadow used under the bottom eyeline defines the eye, but avoid harsh black lines. Blue pencil works on the same principle as the blue in washing powder, so it makes the whites of the eyes seem whiter and more sparkly than ever. Navy mascara has a similar effect. Apply mascara on the bottom lashes first, which avoids 'dotting' on the eyebone. Use two coats on the top lashes, one coat on bottom lashes, allowing mascara to dry in between applications.

Stray hairs should be plucked from eyebrows the day before the wedding and brushed into shape with a little colour. Fair eyebrows need definition with a touch of brow shaper.

Outline lips with pencil or a fine brush, then fill in with colour and blot with a tissue. This stops the lipstick colour seeping. Reapply lip colour and top with a slick of lip gloss, which softens the whole look. Tone lipstick colour and nail polish so they don't clash. Try out a few brands of lipsticks before the wedding to ensure that the one you finally wear is not likely to be the kind that comes off and smudges easily. Expect to do lots of kissing and drinking champagne!

Ideally, treat yourself to a session with a beauty and/or colour consultant, have a relaxing sauna, a massage, or see an aromatherapist before your wedding day. With so much organizing to be done beforehand, it's easy to forget your own needs – especially the need to relax – particularly if you have a demanding job.

Have a rehearsal before the wedding with your hair styled and wearing your headdress and veil. Practise, experiment and feel confident about the look you will create. Let your make-up be special and thought out. It's not the time for clever tricks but for brighter, prettier and fresher effects. In other words, make more of your natural style and be a truly radiant bride.

17

With a Little Bit of Luck

Myths, superstitions and old customs relating to weddings have survived the centuries into our space age, some remarkably intact, though today's bride may not know that blue was deemed a lucky colour or that confetti symbolizes fertility. Paper confetti and rose petals are a modern substitute for rice and corn, the symbol of a full harvest and therefore abundance. The wedding cake has symbolized fertility since Roman times and the custom of the bride cutting the first slice was supposed to ensure a fruitful marriage. Even the old story that luck would befall the couple if they should meet a chimney sweep on their way to church goes back to the days when people believed that soot and ashes were symbols of fertility.

There's something so romantic about very old things and granny's lace has become a fashion trend. While some girls may be lucky enough to inherit a beautiful lace dress from grandma's trunk, or even her veil, most have to be content with a touch of old lace on a handkerchief.

It is traditional for the bride to wear 'something old, something new, something borrowed, something blue'. 'Something old' stands for a link with the past, ensuring that friends will be faithful, and can cover a myriad of things from jewellery to a veil; 'something new' looks to the future, success in a new life; and must be either something newly made or never worn before. 'Something borrowed' is where the family will happily contribute and refers to a link with the present, indicating that the bride takes with her the love of her family. The idea is to borrow something small and perhaps precious – a prayer book, a veil, a piece of jewellery, a hair decoration – but the tradition is said only to be valid if the object is returned after the wedding. Blue is the colour of fidelity and 'something blue' can be worn to be seen, as in a blue trim, sash or flower in the bride's bouquet, or hidden from view in a sexy garter.

Extra luck will be bestowed on the bride who carries a sprig of heather – white to symbolize purity and light – and on the wedding cake there should be a few silver horseshoes, for silver stands for luck and horseshoes for protection against the devil.

A bride should never try on her complete wedding outfit before the wedding day. When trying on a dress in a shop, remove a piece of trimming or the sash and put in the final stitch or tie the last ribbon just before leaving for the church. She must make sure that every pin is removed from her wedding dress when she puts it on, for a single pin left in the folds brings misfortune, 'tis said! But don't be surprised if you find a hair sewn into a handmade dress – to do this is supposed to bring good luck to the seamstress . . .

Rosemary, meaning remembrance and fidelity, was once an important addition to the floral arrangements. It was also part of the bridal wreath, taken by the bride to her new home, where one of the bridesmaids would plant a sprig from the bride's bouquet. If it grew, it would provide rosemary for future daughters' weddings. Another tradition was for a bridesmaid to present a bunch of rosemary, tied with ribbons, to the bridegroom when he arrived at the church.

After the wedding it is the custom to decorate the car and tie an old shoe to it. The origin of this custom is a little obscure but it could date back to Anglo-Saxon times when it was customary for the bride's father to give one of his daughter's shoes to the groom. He then touched his new wife with the tip of the sole to indicate who was master – the authority over the woman having passed from her father to her husband.

There is an old rhyme referring to the lucky colours in which to wed:

Married in white, she has chosen aright
Married in blue, her love will be true
Married in yellow, she'll be ashamed of the fellow
Married in red, she'll wish herself dead
Married in black, she'll wish herself back
Married in grey, she'll travel far away
Married in pink and her spirits will sink
Married in green, she'll be ashamed to be seen.

and about the propitious days for the ceremony:

Monday for health
Tuesday for wealth
Wednesday, the best day of all

Thursday for losses
Friday for crosses
Saturday, no luck at all!

To be married in Lent was not considered propitious:

Marry in Lent
You'll live to repent.

and harvest time was even worse, for you'll 'ne'er survive'.

You and you fiancé should not have surnames of the same initial:

Change the name and not the letter,
Change for the worse not for the better.

If the bride wakes up to the chirping of a bird, that augurs well for married life, but woe betide the bride who breaks anything on her wedding day. And she should never look at herself in the mirror when she is completely ready to leave for the church – have a final check in the mirror but leave just one thing still to put on, however small. Victorian brides completed their dress by adding their gloves at the last moment. The couple should not see each other in their wedding attire until they meet at the altar, but if they should happen to look in the mirror together after the marriage, that is a good sign.

The bridegroom does not have too many superstitions attached to him, but he must not drop his hat nor, especially, the ring. Should the bride have to help him put the ring on her finger he can expect her to be the boss in future. On no account must he go back for anything after the wedding journey has begun, any money he pays out during the day should be in odd sums, and he must ensure that no telegrams are handed to him on the way to church.

Today's bride may be a liberated lady, throwing superstition to the wind, unconcerned with popular myths of the past and especially all those fertility rites – but she'll still toss her bouquet in the hopes that her bridesmaid might catch it and soon be married, as the tradition goes. . . .

18

The Rehearsal

Having a rehearsal for the wedding ceremony is automatic for American church weddings. It is part of the list of traditional things to do and is usually followed by a family meal and get-together. Although it is not as widespread a happening here, it is one that is becoming more popular. There used to be a superstition that the bride should not 'tempt fate' and take part in the rehearsal but should have her matron of honour or chief bridesmaid to stand in for her. Most brides, however, prefer to take a full part in the rehearsal so they are less worried about what to do at the ceremony.

The day or evening preceding the wedding day is usually chosen for the rehearsal of the ceremony, which is held at the church or religious centre where the marriage will take place. All members of the wedding party should be present if possible: the minister, organist or musicians, the bridesmaids, best man, ushers, parents and of course the couple themselves.

It is not necessary to wear the clothes to be worn at the ceremony itself. The idea of a rehearsal is to make sure everyone knows what is expected of them during the service and the minister of religion who will be conducting the following day's ceremony will act as a guide to procedure. It is a time when any problems or questions about the ceremony can be talked about and ironed out, leaving everyone much more relaxed and more able to enjoy and participate fully in the service on the day, instead of concentrating too hard or worrying about what happens next.

For the recessional, the ushers and bridesmaids are often paired to walk together. If their numbers are unequal, the bridesmaids can walk out first, followed by the ushers. (Useful hint – if you save some ribbons from your wedding present packaging you can make a mock bouquet and practise carrying it and passing it at the altar.) During the rehearsal the bride can decide whether she wants her chief bridesmaid or her groom to lift back her veil at the altar.

As several members of both families and all the people fulfilling central roles at the ceremony will be gathered together, it is a pleasant idea to make a special occasion out of the rehearsal and go back to one family home (or the local) for a celebratory drink or meal.

19

The Marriage Ceremony

The main ingredients of most religious wedding services include: prayers of worship and the asking of God for His blessing on the marriage, hymns and psalms, a short address or sermon may be included, marriage vows, other promises and legal requirements, holding of hands and giving of ring(s), signing the register.

Some parts of the wedding service will be the same, whatever church you get married in, for there are certain legal requirements regarding the marriage ceremony. However, there are many variations in order and style, even within churches of the same denomination.

The marriage is a legal ceremony and certain wording may not be altered, but there are ways in which the ceremony can be personalized – by your own choice of music, hymns and certain prayers, for example.

Because marriage is a legal contract, promises have to be made in the presence of a properly registered person and other witnesses. Any marriage taking place in an Anglican church is legal without a registrar being present. A Church of England vicar is registered to conduct weddings. This dates back to the English Marriage Act of 1753 which required all weddings (except those of Jews and Quakers) in England and Wales to take place within buildings of the Church of England and according to its rites. Subsequent Acts of Parliament have modified the rules. The 1898 Act, for example, allowed the governing body of a registered building to arrange for the authorization of a person (often the priest or minister) to register the wedding so that the presence of a civil registrar was no longer needed. Denominations vary in how far they choose to exercise this right, so for some marriages with a religious ceremony it will be necessary for a registrar to be present at the wedding, or alternatively for a separate civil ceremony before a Superintendent Registrar to take place at another time.

There are two statements required by law that the bride and groom must repeat in turn:

'I do solemnly declare that I know not of any lawful impediment why I (say full names) may not be joined in matrimony to (say full names).'

and

'I call upon these persons here present to witness that I (say full names) do take thee (say full names) to be my lawful wedded wife/husband.'

When a marriage takes place in a register office, these vows are made in front of the Superintendent Registrar of the district, and after the signing of the register the newly married couple have their 'marriage lines', so proving they are man and wife according to the law.

Church of England

The ushers should be at the church first, arriving at least 40 minutes before the ceremony is due to start, to guide the guests to their seats and hand out the printed order of service sheets if they are to be used. If you are having bell-ringing, the bells will peal for about a quarter of an hour and the organist will play introductory music while the guests are arriving and being seated. The guests should aim to arrive about ten to fifteen minutes before the time stated on the invitation. The bride's family and friends sit on the left-hand side of the aisle and altar, the groom's family and friends on the right-hand side. The front pews on either side are occupied by the bride and groom's parents, the following pews by their grandparents, close relatives, special guests, and the remainder for friends.

The bridegroom and best man should arrive about twenty minutes before the bride is due and take their places at the top of the aisle. If church fees have not been paid the best man can do that at this point. The bride's mother should arrive about ten minutes before the ceremony is due to begin as should the bridesmaids. The bride's mother will be escorted to her pew by an usher specially detailed to do the honours. The groom's parents should be shown a similar courtesy. The bride's mother, however, should be the last person to take her seat, a few minutes before the ceremony will begin. She makes sure there is a seat beside her for her husband to join her after giving away the bride.

The bride should be on time – even a minute or

THE PROCESSION

Choir Stalls

Groom & Best man

Pews

Groom's mother & father
Groom's grandparents
Groom's relatives
Groom's special guests
Groom's friends

Altar

Minister
Bride's father & Bride
(page)
Chief Bridesmaid
Bridesmaids
Bridesmaids
Best man

Choir Stalls

Pews

Bride's mother & space for bride's father
Bride's grandparents
Bride's relatives
Bride's special guests
Bride's friends

Bride's father

AT THE ALTAR

Altar

Minister
Bride   Groom
(page)
Chief Bridesmaid
Bridesmaids

Bride's father

two early, as the photographer will want to take some photographs of her and her father and a few moments will be needed for her dress to be arranged or any last-minute adjustments to be made to the veil.

As the organist changes from the introductory to the entrance music, the bride takes her father's right arm and leads the procession to the altar, with the bridesmaids and attendants taking their places in couples in the procession. The officiating clergy and sometimes the choir may meet the bride and her father at the door and precede them up the aisle, or the minister may wait for them at the chancel steps.

When the bridal party approaches, the groom and best man take their places on the bride's right at the chancel steps. The chief bridesmaid moves forward to take the bride's bouquet. If there are no bridesmaids the bride gives her bouquet to her father, who may hand it to her mother.

At this point the minister will begin the ceremony. The Prayer Book was authorized in 1662 and, while the language is a little old-fashioned, it is considered by many to be beautiful, solemn and moving. An up-to-date alternative to the traditional marriage service, published in the Alternative Service Book has been in use since 1977 and the language is modern and easier to understand. Between the two, there is the service in the 1928 Prayer Book. Which version is used should be the subject of discussion long before the actual ceremony.

The wedding ceremony begins with an introduction explaining the church's view of marriage and what Christian marriage is all about – that it was given by God, blessed by Christ, and is a symbol of Christ's relationship with his church. This is followed by the section concerned with the approach to marriage: marriage should not be approached inadvisedly (rashly), lightly (without due thought), wantonly (recklessly) or to satisfy lust but reverently (with due respect), discreetly (after consideration), advisedly (deliberately), soberly (with serious purpose) and in the fear of God.

The purposes of marriage are then detailed – to have children, to avoid immorality, to give each other companionship (mutual society), help and comfort. The alternative service lists the purposes of marriage as being to comfort and help each other; to know each other in love, united in body, heart and life – and to have children.

The core of the ceremony, the exchange of promises, is in four parts:

1. 'Is there any impediment to the marriage?' – if any reason is known for the marriage not to take place, it must be stated now.

2. 'Wilt thou have?' – the question is asked of the bridegroom first, and then the bride, and they say 'I will' when asked to love, comfort, honour and keep myself for him/her. The promise to 'serve and obey' is not often used now, but the bride will be asked if she wishes to say those words within her promises.

3. 'I take thee' – the right hands of the bride and groom are joined and in turn they repeat their promises to each other. They promise: to have and to hold, for better for worse, for richer for poorer, in

sickness and in health, to love and to cherish till death do us part, according to God's holy ordinance. Although the Prayer Book service only refers to the giving of the ring by the groom to the bride and the placing of it on her finger, if the couple wish to exchange rings the minister will usually give the bride the opportunity of placing a ring on her groom's finger. The groom gives his promise to share with his bride all that he is and all that he owns. Many couples prefer to use the word 'share' rather than endow.

4. 'Those whom God hath joined together let no man put asunder' and with this declaration the couple are now man and wife and the register can be signed.

The bride's father is present with the couple at the altar steps until he has completed his role – that of giving his daughter's hand in marriage to the bridegroom – after which he can step back into the front pew to join his wife. The best man's role is completed after he has handed over the ring(s), which are blessed by the minister. He can then step slightly aside from the group.

After the ceremony the bridal party moves to the vestry, where the marriage register is signed by the bride (in her maiden name), the groom and two witnesses (often the best man and chief bridesmaid). The procession to the vestry, where the marriage register is signed, is led by the minister, followed by the bride and groom, groom's father and bride's mother, bride's father with groom's mother, best man and chief bridesmaid, then the bridesmaids. Other members of the close family may also join the procession.

Coming out of the church, the ushers may be part of the procession and accompany the adult bridesmaids, but this will depend on personal choice and arrangements. After the couple's relatives have left their pews, they can be followed from the church by the special guests and then by friends.

Nonconformist churches

Most of the services held in Nonconformist churches follow a similar pattern to one another. Although the actual wording and order of service may differ slightly, the contents are very similar.

The United Reform Church

During the Order for a Wedding Service the minister calls on the congregation to worship and pray and reminds those present that they are gathered together in the presence of God as witnesses to a wedding and to rejoice and support the couple with their prayers. He reviews the purpose of marriage – a gift and calling of God not to be entered upon lightly but responsibly, and in obedience to the Gospel of Christ, provided by God for the companionship of help and comfort in mutual care, for faithfulness, love and mutual honour, for the nurture of children and the enrichment of society.

Legal declarations (in the presence of the authorized person or Registrar and two witnesses) are made to state that neither of the couple knows of

COMING OUT OF THE CHURCH

| Altar |

Bride's father & Groom's mother
Groom's father & Bride's mother
Bridesmaid & Bridesmaid
Bridesmaid & Bridesmaid
Best man & Chief Bridesmaid
(page)
Bridegroom & Bride

Pews
Bride's grandparents
Bride's relatives

Bride's special guests
Bride's special friends
Bride's friends

Pews
Groom's grandparents
Groom's relatives

Groom's special guests
Groom's special friends
Groom's friends

any reasons why they should not legally marry, and an address; readings or prayers may be said before the couple make their promises to love, comfort, honour and protect, in times of prosperity and health and in times of trouble and suffering and be faithful as long as they live.

The minister asks who is giving the bride away. The couple's right hands are joined and they in turn, the bridegroom first, call upon those present to witness their vows. The minister then takes the ring(s), giving it (one) to the bridegroom who places it on the bride's finger saying that the ring is given in God's name as a symbol of all that they will share together. If they are exchanging rings, the bride will say the same words to her bridegroom as she places the ring on his finger. If there is only one ring she may say that she receives the ring in God's name and as a symbol of their sharing.

The minister then declares the couple to be man and wife, adding, 'what God has joined together, man must not separate', and gives the couple the Marriage Blessing.

A variety of prayers and readings may be used at various parts of the ceremony depending on the minister and couple's wishes.

Certain United Reform churches have authorized persons, of whom the minister is usually one, and they are able to conduct weddings and fill in and keep the marriage registers. In other churches they do not avail themselves of this right and need to have a civil registrar present. The legal requirements will be discussed with the couple at the time they approach the minister to discuss their future wedding.

Methodist

As with the United Reform churches, it should be discussed with the minister of the specific church whether it is registered for the solemnization of marriages without the presence of a registrar.

The Methodist Marriage Service is very similar to the one outlined above, with a declaration of the purpose of marriage and legal declarations as to their being no impediments, prayers and readings, the vows, the giving or exchanging of rings when the couple pledge themselves to each other in the name of the Holy Trinity, the pronouncement of the marriage, a prayer of intercession and thanksgiving and the blessing.

A couple who have already been married by a civil ceremony in a register office can request a minister to read the Marriage Service (though probably without repeating the vows which have already been made) or to perform the 'Service for the blessing of the Marriage previously solemnized'. He must first see the Certificate of Marriage.

During a Service of Blessing the couple stand in front of the minister, the wife on the left-hand side of her husband. There is a Declaration of Purpose, in which the minister speaks of the meaning of marriage according to the teaching of Christ – a lifelong union of love. Prayers are said and some readings from scripture are made.

The minister asks the husband and wife whether, since they have taken each other as lawful wedded wife/husband and wish to acknowledge before God that they desire their married life to be according to His will, they will love, honour, keep and be faithful to one another as long as they both live. Each replies that with God's help they will. A prayer is said over the ring(s) and the couple join their right hands and together acknowledge that God has bound them together in Christian marriage for the rest of their lives. There follows a blessing and prayers of intercession, thanksgiving and praise.

The service of Blessing is not used for the solemnization of a marriage and is not recorded in the marriage register.

Roman Catholic

In some parishes the priest has arranged for himself or a parishioner to be authorized to register marriages, but this is not always so. In any case, the couple must give due notice of intention to marry to the registrar of their district(s). They should first meet the priest, preferably at least two to three months before the planned wedding, who usually refers the couple to the local register office and civil requirements are dealt with and arranged there. He will want to see copies of your baptismal and confirmation certificates. Banns are published three times in your local parish church(es), but if only one of the couple is a Catholic, banns will not be read.

The belief of members of the Catholic Church is that marriage is a sacrament (one of seven sacraments). The marriage service is combined with the celebration of Mass and called Nuptial Mass. If one of the couple to be married is not a Catholic it may be decided to have the marriage rite alone and not continue with the Mass.

The priest may meet the bridal procession at the door of the church and lead them up the aisle, or alternatively may greet them at the altar. The service begins, as with Mass, with prayers and the Act of Penance followed by readings from the Bible in the Liturgy of the Word. The Marriage Rite follows, during which the priest asks the couple if they freely undertake the obligations of marriage, to state that there is no legal impediment to the marriage, and to declare their consent before God and His Church.

With their right hands joined (the bride's hand may be placed in the bridegroom's hand by her father) they make their vows. The ring(s), signs of love and fidelity, are blessed and exchanged. Prayers and the Creed are said, after which the civil register can be signed.

If a Nuptial Mass is not being celebrated, the priest may conclude the service with a blessing. A Mass will continue with the Liturgy of the Eucharist and the Communion Rite and conclude with a blessing.

Religious Society of Friends (Quakers)

The basis of a Friends marriage today is much the same as it was in the early days of the Society. It has been kept simple, and a meeting for worship for the solemnization of marriage is held in the same form as a meeting for worship at other times. An announcement of the intended marriage is given at your local Sunday meeting(s).

Friends have their own local registering officer who is legally allowed to witness the marriage and the signing of the certificate, but notice of intention to marry must still be given by the couple to the Superintendent Registrar of their district(s) and a certificate or certificate and licence obtained.

At the Meeting the couple stand, hold hands and declare one after the other and before other Friends that they take each other to be their wife/husband, promising that, with God's help, they will be loving and faithful as long as they both live. A certificate is signed during the Meeting by the couple and by at least two of those present as witnesses, and is read aloud by the registering officer. Rings may be exchanged but they are not part of the religious ceremony.

Jewish ceremony

The couple must both be of the Jewish faith to marry according to Jewish law.

The normal synagogue marriage is both a civil and religious ceremony. Two separate applications for permission to marry are required, at the Superintendent Registrar's office of the district(s) in which the couple live(s) and a certificate or certificate and licence obtained as well as at the Office of the Chief Rabbi or Religious Authority under which the ceremony is taking place. Ministers of synagogues are empowered to register the marriage civilly. There are certain dates on which marriages cannot take place, including the Sabbath and fast days. The details of the ceremony may differ slightly from synagogue to synagogue and for those members of a Reform synagogue as distinct from those of the Orthodox faith.

On the Sabbath before the wedding the bridegroom is called to the Torah. It is customary for the bride and groom to fast on the day of the wedding until after the ceremony.

Etiquette at a synagogue can vary, although the groom is expected to arrive first. Usually he sits in the Warden's box with his father, future father-in-law and best man. The groom takes his place first under the *chuppah*, (a canopy representing the new home the couple are about to build together).

The bride is usually brought in by her father, followed by bridesmaids, the bride's mother escorted (often by a male relative) and bridegroom's parents. It is an old Jewish custom, however, that the bride is brought in by her mother and future mother-in-law.

Before the bride comes under the *chuppah* the groom is formally requested by the minister to give his approval to the appointment of two witnesses of the *ketubah* and his acceptance of the terms and conditions of the *ketubah*, whereby he undertakes a number of basic obligations towards his wife.

The bride stands under the *chuppah* at the groom's right and at each side of the *chuppah* stand the *unterfuhrers*, those who have conducted the couple to the *chuppah*, usually the parents of the couple. An address or special prayers and psalms may be offered. Two blessings are recited over a cup of wine, known as the 'blessings of betrothal'.

In Jewish law the couple become husband and wife

when the man takes the ring and places it on his bride's finger. Her acceptance of it signifies consent. The ring is placed on the bride's right index finger but after the service she may transfer it to the 'ring finger'. The groom recites a declaration in Hebrew, 'Behold, thou are consecrated unto me by this ring, according to the law of Moses and of Israel'.

The *ketubah* is read and handed to the bride and there follow the seven blessings of marriage. At the conclusion of both the bethrothal and the marriage blessings, the couple sip wine to symbolize that from henceforth they must share the same cup of life, sweet or otherwise.

A glass is broken by the bridegroom, a custom that originally expressed mourning at the loss of the Temple and today is a reminder that marital happiness can be shattered by one simple and decisive act but putting the pieces back together again is not so simple. The ceremony is concluded by the minister pronouncing the ancient priestly blessing. The various marriage documents are signed and the couple usually spend a few moments together in a private room (*yihud*) denoting their newly acquired status as husband and wife entitled to live together.

Double Weddings

Sometimes two members of a family, or two very close friends, may plan to marry around the same time, and decide on a double wedding, thus saving on the costs of two receptions and the work they entail.

For a double wedding at a register office, both

couples have to apply for a licence or certificate in the usual way. To marry in church, the banns will be posted in the parishes of each individual member of the wedding group.

The invitations come from the parents of the brides, with the elder sister, sister of a brother, or elder of two girls named first in the invitation. Her parents are also named first. Each bride has bridesmaids or pageboys – preferably both choosing the same number of each – and each groom has his own best man and ushers. While the brides will naturally wear different dresses, their veils and trains should be of a similar length, style and formality. The bridesmaids will be dressed differently, but in colours that co-ordinate and harmonize.

At the church, the respective parents will have to decide who will sit in the front pew, or whether they will share it. The groom of the first bride stands in the centre of the aisle with his best man on his right.

The two brides travel in separate cars. The bride named first in the invitation will be the first to go into the church, escorted by her father or the person who is giving her away. She leads the procession to the altar, followed by her attendants. Behind her comes the second bride and her attendants. If the brides are sisters, the second bride may be escorted up the aisle by a close family member, who will move away when her father takes over to give her away. At the altar, the two couples will stand side by side. The attendants of the first bride stand to the left, those of the second bride to the right. The father stands by his elder daughter in a double wedding for sisters.

The ceremony is the same for a normal wedding, but the responses and vows for each couple will be said in turn. The final blessing may be a joint one.

On leaving the church, the first couple is followed by the second couple and then by their respective attendants. The first bride's mother is escorted by the first groom's father, then comes the first bride's father and the first groom's mother. And so on. If the brides are sisters, the best man and a close family member or friend can stand in for the parents of the second bride and escort her groom's parents down the aisle.

After the photographs have been taken, the two couples take separate cars and drive to a shared reception.

20

The Bridesmaids

The chief bridesmaid (called matron of honour if she is married) generally assists the bride and offers practical and moral support. She may help to choose the wedding dress and trousseau if the bride so wishes and also helps the bride dress before the wedding. She leaves for the church before the bride so she can meet her at the church porch and there makes sure her dress and veil are arranged neatly. As the bride walks up the aisle on her father's arm the chief bridesmaid follows her and takes her bouquet at the altar. For the signing of the register she takes the arm of the best man and walks behind the bride and groom to the vestry. She is often a witness at the signing of the register, and leaves the church in the recessional with the best man. She generally looks after the other bridesmaids and pages during the day, assists the bride in any way she can at the reception and then helps her to change into her going-away clothes. She (or the bride's mother) takes charge of the bridal wear after the bride has changed and delivers it later to an agreed place. She may also be helpful to the couple when they return from honeymoon, helping them settle into their new home. The person who fills the role of chief bridesmaid is usually either an adult sister or close female friend of the bride.

All the other bridesmaids really have to do is complement the bride, smile and look decorative and pretty. They follow the bride and may help her with her train if she has one. Their dresses should be as formal or informal as the bride's dress to make the picture complete. Bridesmaids dress more or less identically while the chief bridesmaid or matron of honour may wear a different colour. A small brides-maid can wear a younger version of the adults' clothes. Shoes are often dyed to match the dresses. Gloves and headdresses are optional.

The bridesmaids usually pay for their own dresses, and in this case the bride should choose a style and material that could be worn again on another occa-sion after the wedding. Suggested styles include simply cut dresses or long shirts for adult brides-maids, pretty summer dresses or velvet pinafore dresses for children. When the bride chooses dresses that are unlikely to have future use, she should pay for them. Traditionally it is the bride's father who pays for the attendants' attire but as costs soar many of the traditional boundaries on payment are break-ing down and most people are happy to share costs wherever possible, as a sign of friendship.

While bridesmaids don't want to compete with the bride on her wedding day they will certainly want to complement her by looking pretty and at their best. There is more to planning the overall look of the wedding party than simply making sure the attend-ants' dresses don't clash. The whole party is going to be seen together at the church and in the photographs so it is worth some extra attention to detail in creating a co-ordinating look for the group.

This is just as true for a register office wedding as for one in a religious setting. For a register office wedding a chief bridesmaid as such is often not dressed in the same way as for a church wedding, but the bride will still need some moral support from a good adult friend or sister, someone who will be close to her and dressed well. So colours and styles will need to be discussed and planned beforehand. A small child wearing a pretty party dress is often part of the wedding group at the register office.

If possible, it is best to buy all the bridesmaids' dresses in the same shop, or have them made by the same person. If the bride's dress is plain white, a shade picked from the colours of the flowers in her bouquet is often chosen for the bridesmaids' attire, or if the dress has a coloured trim the bridesmaids' dresses could be in a material of a similar shade. If the bridesmaids are to be dressed alike, choose a colour that will suit all the girls – and a style that will flatter them all, too, bearing in mind that sizes and figures may vary enormously.

Being on show as a bridesmaid means that make-up, too, is important, and it is a good idea for the bride and her adult attendants to go along together to a beauty expert, perhaps in the local department store, to choose eye and lip colours that will complement each other, as well as the dresses. As each person will have different skin tones and hair colouring, identical make-up is not possible, but shades can be chosen that will suit each individual while not clashing with another bridesmaid. It is best to keep to subtle, pretty shades – harsh lines and strong colours seldom look good with bridal fashions.

The bride will be planning her hairstyle well in advance of the wedding and the bridesmaids, too, will have to decide how their hair will look and if they will be wearing any form of headdress, such as a single flower, ribbons, a hat or coronet or whether they will be relying totally on a pretty hairstyle. It is a good idea to plan a style with a hairdresser beforehand and have a trial cut. Attendants' hairstyles need not be identical; they can be similar while still suiting their own individual style of looks.

Child attendants are always scene-stealers and look attractive in the bridal party. They can wear a pretty party dress or small pinafore that can be teamed afterwards with a different blouse or poloneck jumper. Boys could wear a velvet suit or sailor-suit style or it is often possible to hire special pageboy suits. As with adult bridesmaids the children should wear similar styles and colours designed to co-ordinate with the colour scheme of the wedding party.

The bridesmaids' posies or baskets of flowers look best when made up in shades and colours taken from the bride's bouquet or, if the bride is only carrying a prayer book, in colours that go with the dresses they are wearing. If the bridesmaids are to be given a piece of jewellery as a present they may wish to wear it at the ceremony.

Bridesmaids are usually younger sisters of the bride and/or groom (do choose from both families) or cousins, godchildren or children of close friends. All the bridesmaids can, of course, be adults (but unmarried). Think very, very carefully about choosing children under the age of five . . .

Pageboys perform the same duties as small bridesmaids, and are usually younger brothers, nephews or godchildren.

21

The Bridegroom's Role

The bridegroom tends to get rather left out in all the preparations and planning, and even on the day of the wedding he plays a supporting role among the cast. His bride is definitely the star of the day – and her mother the understudy and organizer – and yet he's usually the one who starts the whole show when he plucks up the courage to propose! He may even have had to go through the whole ordeal of asking the bride's father for his daughter's hand in marriage. Then he has to pay for the engagement ring and wedding ring, though he usually doesn't get to choose them.

So what does the bridegroom have to do, other than be at the church in time? He chooses his best man and ushers and makes sure both he and they are suitably attired. He goes with his fiancée to choose an engagement and wedding ring and pays for them, and maybe to choose a wedding ring for himself (which the bride buys).

He gives the money for the best man to pay church fees, including the licence, banns, wedding certificate, service, verger, organist and choir and buys presents for the bride, bridesmaids, best man and ushers. In the floral department he pays for the flowers for the bride, bridesmaids, bride's mother and his mother, and buttonholes for the best man and himself. He also pays for the transport for himself and his best man to the church and for himself and his bride to and from the reception. Traditionally he pays for the honeymoon, but today most wives share this as they would any other holiday.

For a wedding in a register office his costs will be similar, but he will only have to pay for the marriage licence and certificate plus the registrar's fees instead of church fees, and there are likely to be fewer presents to buy.

Because the best man has a lot of responsibilities it is important that the groom chooses someone he can rely on. A brother or close friend is normally chosen.

Stag nights are fun and pure tradition, but are preferably held a day or two before the eve of the wedding if the groom is going to be in any state at all to cope with the proceedings.

Together with his bride, the groom arranges to see the minister of religion or goes to the Superintendant Registrar's office to discuss the form of service or licence and to arrange the date of the wedding. Although in most cases it is not necessary for both the bride and groom to appear at the registrar's office to arrange the licence, it is a happy occasion that can be shared. The bridegroom should also discuss the wedding and honeymoon arrangements with his bride – again it is nice to go together to the travel agent – and of course decide where they will live and plan the new home.

With all the planning and thought that goes into what the bride is going to wear, the groom should be planning his attire, too. If the wedding is to be a formal one in church he is likely to be wearing a morning suit, and will need to go for a fitting when hiring the suit. This should be arranged in good time in case alterations have to be made and also to ensure the style and colour chosen will be available on the day.

The other alternative for most men is a smart lounge suit, preferably of the type that can be worn again on other occasions. Some men choose a white suit for a register office wedding. If shoes are new, don't forget to check for labels on the sole!

On the day of the wedding the groom has to make sure he arrives (with his best man) in good time at the church. Together they sit in the front right-hand pew in front of the altar and wait for the bride to arrive. It is a nice gesture for the groom to turn to the bride as she approaches the altar and give her an encouraging smile – after all, while he has had umpteen pairs of eyes staring at his back, she has had to face them head on as well as having that long walk in a dress she is not accustomed to, and is probably somewhat shaky.

Neither the bride nor the groom have to say too much during the ceremony, but the vows are very important and everyone wants to hear them. So the groom needs to rehearse, be determined not to stutter and to say them in a good clear voice – despite the nerves.

Then there is the procession to the vestry and back through the church. Everyone gets camera happy at this point and the groom gets some idea of what it could be like to be a star; then he takes his bride along to the reception and to shake hands with all the guests and has a much better idea of how Prince Philip feels.

At the reception, if it is a formal one with a top table, the bride and groom sit together at the centre of the table, the bride on the groom's left with the bride's father next to the bride. If it is an informal reception buffet or cocktail party, the bride and groom move around among the guests, chatting, until it is time to cut the cake, when they are both once more at centre stage.

The bride and groom together cut the cake – her hand on the knife first, then his hand over hers, and finally the bride's other hand on top.

The groom has to make a speech. The bride doesn't (though she may choose to). It is best to keep it short and thank everyone – and it is usual to comment on how pretty all the women look (and particularly the bride).

Eventually it is time to get organized to leave the party and set off on honeymoon (if there is to be one). If he is wearing formal dress or morning suit, then the groom goes to change at the same time as the bride and reappears in the male version of 'going-away clothes', usually a suit or well cut jacket and trousers.

At this point, all the well-wishers can be left behind and the groom can get on with playing a new role – that of husband.

22

The Best Man

The best man, who is usually a brother or close friend of the groom, has a very important role to play at the wedding. He must be dependable for he is the chief organizer, friend and helper to the groom and is often chosen as a witness at the wedding. As well as doing plenty of practical things on the day before the wedding, the best man will be very useful if he manages to soothe away some of the pre-wedding nerves. (And that does not mean getting the bride-groom drunk the night before!) In fact, a good best man ensures that the stag night party is held at least a couple of nights before the wedding and that the groom gets a good night's rest before the ceremony. However, a small drink before getting off to church might calm a few ruffled nerves. Although there is no best man at a register office wedding, a brother or close friend will be needed to fulfil the role at the reception.

On the purely practical side, here's a checklist for the best man of things to do to make sure the wedding day is as problem-free as possible:

The day before

- Check that the florist has the order for the button-hole flowers for the bridegroom and best man, and ushers.
- If suits are being hired, check that they will be ready for collection on the day or preferably collect them the day before.
- Make sure everything that is to be worn on the day, for the bridegroom and best man, is ready in the wardrobe.
- See that the ring is easily accessible and won't be forgotten.
- Contact the taxi/hire car company and make sure they have the order for the required number of cars, the time and place. The best man arranges for the cars to take himself and the groom to church, the bride and groom to the reception and the best man and bridesmaids to the reception.
- If a taxi is to take the bridal couple from the reception to a honeymoon destination, airport or station, this should also have been booked and the booking double-checked the day before.
- If hire cars are not used and you are relying on friends' cars, phone to check their cars are still available for the day.
- Get together with the groom, check all travel plans, hotel reservations, tickets, travellers' cheques, passports, etc. Make sure they are all kept together and in order.
- Make sure the bridegroom has packed his suit-cases, and arrange for the cases (his and the bride's) to be at the reception venue, if they are

leaving for their honeymoon from there. If they are staying at a local hotel overnight, have the suitcases taken there.

- Collect the Order of Service sheets from the bride's mother, for distribution at the church just before the service.
- Meet the ushers and discuss with them the seating arrangements in the church.
- If the wedding presents are to be displayed, the bride's family may need some help with this.
- Get the money for the church fees from the groom and pay them, or have it ready to pay on the morning before the ceremony.
- Reassure the groom – and persuade him to have an early, quiet night. Stag parties, drinking too much and practical jokes aren't funny when the 'morning after the night before' is your wedding day.

On the day

- If hire suits have not already been collected, collect them first thing and deliver the bridegroom's suit and accessories.
- Collect the buttonholes from the florist if they are not to be delivered.
- Get dressed for the wedding.
- Go to the bridegroom's home and help him dress for the wedding.
- Put the wedding ring in a waistcoat pocket – and remember which pocket it is in.
- Take charge of the travel documents, collected together the day before.

- Take charge of the suitcases for the honeymoon.
- Make sure the bridegroom has packed his 'going-away' clothes separately, and take charge of that suitcase.
- If there is time for the best man to take the suitcases to the place of the reception he should take them there, otherwise make sure an usher has been delegated to do this.
- Get to the church, with the bridegroom, about fifteen minutes before the bride is due – take traffic problems into consideration when planning the journey time.
- Try to be as relaxed a companion as possible for the bridegroom.
- Pay the church fees if not already done.
- At the church, walk with the bridegroom to the pew at the foot of the chancel steps and sit on his right-hand side.
- Hand over the ring at the ordained time in the service.
- Offer your left arm to the chief bridesmaid, then follow the bridal couple and go to the vestry after the service, to sign the marriage register as a witness.
- Hand the bridegroom his hat and gloves as they leave the church.
- Help to organize the wedding party for the photographer at the church door.
- Usher the bride and groom into their car.
- Take the bridesmaids to the reception.
- Help to guide the guests to the receiving line.
- See the guests are correctly seated.
- Act as toastmaster/master of ceremonies.

- Reply to the toast of 'the bridesmaids'.
- Read out the telegrams.
- Give the groom his travel documents as the couple change to go away.
- See the couple and their luggage to their car or taxi.
- Return to the guests at the reception, see them on their way. If required, escort the bridesmaids home.
- Collect the groom's wedding suit and, if hired, return it promptly.
- If wedding presents have been displayed, help to transport them.

23

The Ushers

The main job of the men delegated to be ushers is to seat the wedding guests at the church. They should arrive at least 40 minutes before the ceremony is due to begin, and hand out order of service sheets as the guests arrive. They escort the women guests to their pews, asking whether they are friends of the bride or groom. The bride's family and friends sit on the left, those of the groom's on the right of the church. The woman's escort follows a few steps behind her. Male guests follow the usher to the pew.

One usher is usually specifically asked to seat the bride and groom's mothers and very close family such as grandparents. This is usually the chief usher. If any of the groom's brothers are acting as ushers they may be delegated to seat certain members of the family. Ushers also hand service sheets and/or hymn books to the guests.

After the ceremony the ushers will escort the bridesmaids from the church and see that all guests have transport to the reception. At the reception the ushers mix with the guests and see that no one is left standing alone.

All the male members of the wedding party dress alike. If it is a formal wedding the ushers will have to hire formal dress, otherwise they will match the groom's attire – dark suit or smart lounge suit. Their ties should match or at least be similar. All the hire clothes should come from the same shop to ensure uniformity. The ushers usually pay their own hire charges. They will be given a buttonhole flower by the groom.

Ushers are usually relatives or close friends of the groom.

24

The Reception

The reception is one of the first things to be planned, once the date, time and place of the wedding ceremony have been decided on. There is a fair amount of organizing to be done – the amount is usually in relation to the type of celebration you have in mind.

There are many types of reception that can be held, but it will probably depend on how big you want the party to be, how many guests you plan to invite, and your finances. The reception is usually the most expensive part of the whole wedding day.

Choices for the venue include the bride's parents' home and/or garden, a hotel, restaurant or club or church hall. Guests may be offered cocktail snacks, a buffet or a full sit-down meal. The time of the ceremony often dictates the type of reception. A formal sit-down meal or buffet usually follows a late-morning wedding; a ceremony in the church in the early afternoon would be followed by a finger buffet or lavish tea, while for a late afternoon wedding the reception may begin with drinks, followed by a sit-down dinner with a dance or disco.

Several alternatives to the traditional reception have gained favour and popularity in the last few years. These include a meal in a restaurant for a small group of people immediately after a register office wedding (which in many cases is followed by a big party in the couple's home after they have returned from honeymoon) or a meal at a hotel or at the bride's parents' home for close family and older relatives, held after the ceremony, with a disco party on the evening of the wedding for the couple's friends. Many couples, too, decide not to go on honeymoon from the reception, especially when it is held in the evening, but to stay to the end of the party and spend their wedding night in a nearby hotel.

Another tradition that is rapidly changing concerns the heavy decision about 'who pays?' Traditionally, the answer is 'the bride's father', but with the very high cost involved, especially of a big reception with plenty to eat and drink for a large number of guests, the final bill can be crippling. Today, many people choose to share costs: the bridegroom's family offers to pay half, or at least make a good contribution, and the couple themselves if they can afford it usually make a contribution too. Some couples opt to pay the whole cost themselves.

Formal reception

The bride and groom and both sets of parents leave the church first so they are ready to receive their guests as they arrive. A receiving line may seem over-formal but it does give everyone a chance of meeting, however briefly. Guests can thank the bride's parents, kiss and compliment the bride and congratulate the bridegroom, then quickly pass on to join the other guests and drink a glass of sherry or wine. The other guests and drink a glass of sherry or wine. The receiving line consists of the bride's mother, bride's father, groom's mother, groom's father, bride and groom.

When a set meal has been chosen there is usually a 'top table' for the celebrities of the day, positioned where they can be seen, and later heard, by everyone in the room. The bride and groom sit at the centre of the table, the bride on the groom's left. Next to the bride sits her father, who has the groom's mother next to him. On the bridegroom's right he has the bride's mother, who sits next to the groom's father. A top table, then, may look similar to this:

Bridesmaid | Best man | Groom's mother | Bride's father | Bride | Groom | Bride's mother | Groom's father | Chief Bridesmaid | Chief Usher

Bridesmaid [cake] Usher

If the bride's parents are divorced and have remarried, the top table could be thus:

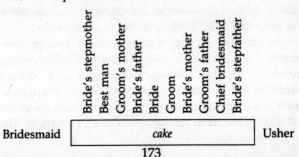

Bride's stepmother | Best man | Groom's mother | Bride's father | Bride | Groom | Bride's mother | Groom's father | Chief bridesmaid | Bride's stepfather

Bridesmaid [cake] Usher

Top tables can be a moveable feast depending on family needs and relationships. However, the bride and groom should always be in the centre and have close family members seated beside them. It is still the convention that married couples do not sit beside each other at formal receptions.

The guests at the reception may be seated at long tables adjoining the top table, to make a U-shape, or there may be tables seating small groups. When a seating plan has been made and named place cards are used it is advisable for both mothers to get together and ensure that everyone is seated next to someone they like. It is not a good idea to extend family feuds or dislikes at a wedding. At a sit-down reception, there is less opportunity for guests to circulate and mingle, so seating takes on a particular importance. At some wedding receptions all the guests of the bride and her family are seated together at a few tables and all the guests of the groom and his family are seated together at other tables; at others, the two families' guests are intermingled. This is purely a matter of choice, but it would seem preferable that at least a few people on each table know each other so communication is easier.

It is during the second half of the meal that the toasts and speeches are made. They should be brief and informal. The bride's father (or favourite uncle or close family friend) makes a short speech and proposes a toast to the bride and groom. The bridegroom replies and proposes a toast to the bridesmaids, to which the best man replies and then goes on to read the telegrams and cards of good wishes.

If the bride and groom cut the cake before the

toasts start, it can be taken away and cut into small pieces, to be handed to guests after the speeches have finished.

Dancing can begin at any time after the cake has been cut and the speeches made. The bride and groom are the first to take the floor and after a short time 'centre stage' dancing together, the couple part so the bride can dance with her father and father-in-law and the groom can dance with his mother and mother-in-law, while the best man dances with the chief bridesmaid and the ushers dance with the bridesmaids. After all the people from the top table have danced, the other guests may join in.

The bride and groom should spend time circulating among their guests, to chat and thank them for the presents.

Informal receptions

When there is to be a buffet meal or cocktail snacks, sandwiches and canapés, the traditional reception formalities are less rigid. The reception line is usually kept, however, as this does ensure that everyone has at least a few words with bride, groom and their close families.

Going away

If the bride and groom are leaving the reception to go on honeymoon, they go to change into their 'going-away' clothes about an hour or so after the cake has been cut and the toasts given, or at a time to suit their travel arrangements.

The chief bridesmaid goes to help the bride, and the best man to help the groom. The best man should check that the luggage hasn't been touched since he put the locked suitcases away for safe keeping. Stories about newlyweds and what they find in their suitcases when opened on honeymoon are legion!

It is traditional for the bride before she goes to change to throw her bouquet to a bridesmaid or unmarried female guest, and her garter to the unmarried men at the party. Brides who want to keep their bouquet, or to give it to an elderly relative, can toss a single flower from it – or a posy bought for the purpose – and still keep the tradition going.

Planning the reception

All the possible venues for holding a reception party have their advantages and disadvantages. Church halls, town halls or local assembly rooms are usually more suitable for an informal or semi-formal wedding reception, while catering establishments such as restaurants, banqueting halls, private clubs and hotel banqueting and reception rooms are more often used for semi-formal and formal receptions. Private homes, depending on their size and facilities can be used for any type of reception. The final choice of location will depend on many factors, including number of guests, budget, the nature and form of the ceremony (a formal wedding should be followed by a formal reception), availability and how much work and organization whoever is giving the reception is prepared to do.

Having a reception at home may give more flexibility but is likely to involve more organization, whether the party is to be formal or informal. Local caterers can be brought in, or family and friends can have a cooking and baking spree for weeks before the wedding, choosing mainly food that can easily be frozen beforehand and defrosted on the day it is needed. Adequate seating and cloakroom facilities will be required and there may be a good deal of equipment that will need to be hired. Although a home reception will require a lot of hard work and attention to detail it is most rewarding when everyone says how successful the event has been.

The advantage of hiring a hall is that many details are taken care of, for most places will provide enough seating, tables, and bar equipment and will have sufficient cloakrooms and kitchen facilities. However, you will still have to organize the food and catering arrangements, the wedding cake, decoration and entertainment. Hired halls rarely lend themselves to formal wedding receptions and some can be quite dingy and uninspiring but, with a bit of thought and helpful friends, they can be decorated and brightened up. You need some good imaginative ideas and friends who are happy to do some work to make the setting attractive. Atmosphere is very important. In a hired hall, you'll need lots of flowers – big bowls around the room, posies on tables – prettily decorated tables, a good colour scheme, suitable music. Make sure the caterers can cope with available facilities. If you are doing the catering you'll need lots of helpers and to be an excellent organizer.

If you live near a river or canal, consider hiring a boat. If you want an unusual venue for the reception, check advertisements in local newspapers and bridal magazines, or enquire at the town hall whether they have a list of suggestions. But make absolutely sure the facilities are adequate for your needs.

Hotels and restaurants can usually provide all the services required and many hotels have special 'package deals' for wedding receptions, including the use of rooms for changing. Such packages may consist of the choice of a set menu and drinks, the provision of the cake, music, decorations and waitress and bar service. A buffet reception may be offered instead of a set meal. Ask around (personal recommendations are always best), read advertisements, ask for brochures and visit potential venues yourself.

Checkpoints to look for: a good atmosphere, space available, staffing, how busy the hotel is, value for money, attitude of the banqueting manager. Once satisfied on those points, ask some more detailed questions: are flowers and decorations included in the price? Do you have to pay extra for cloakroom attendants? Will you need a toastmaster – if so, a microphone may be necessary and will the venue charge for its hire? What about parking facilities? What is the time limit on the room you want to hire, and is there a charge for hiring a changing room for the bride and groom? What about VAT and service charges – are they included in the quotation and will tips be necessary? If so, to whom?

Choosing the food

Most formal wedding receptions take the form of a three- or four-course sit-down meal with waiter service. Semi-formal receptions usually have a buffet meal and informal receptions will have cocktail style snacks. All will require help with serving the food, collecting plates and clearing up afterwards. A sit-down meal is the most expensive because of the number of courses and staff that are required. A buffet should be less expensive, but this will depend on the choice of buffet food – special delicacies or large entrees will put up the price.

When making enquiries about the probable cost of the meal ask about deposit guarantee, and payment policies of the catering company or establishment. Will corkage be charged if you provide the wine? Ask for a selection of set menus – if you want to substitute a course or a dish, is this possible and will there be an extra charge? Are facilities available for vegetarian meals if you require them? Make sure you both understand the arrangements for drinks – and get everything in writing. Get quotations from several companies or hotels and make careful comparisons before making the final decision, as well as asking around for recommendations and, in the case of restaurants and hotels, visiting them and eating there. Actual menus will differ from place to place and between catering companies and establishments, but the following are fairly typical of traditional set meal and buffet menus for wedding receptions.

Those likely to be the cheapest are listed first under each heading:

Set meals

- Choice of soup, York ham, roast beef or cold roast chicken or turkey, green salad or a mixture of salads and potatoes, rolls and butter, fruit salad and ice cream or peaches and cream or pears Belle Hélène, cheese and biscuits, tea or coffee.
- Soup, roast chicken or turkey, stuffing, potatoes, peas, salad, rolls and butter, fruit salad and cream or apple pie and cream, cheese and biscuits, coffee or tea.
- Prawn cocktail, fresh poached Scotch salmon cutlets, hollandaise sauce, mixed salads, potatoes, rolls and butter, apple pie and cream or gateaux, cheese and biscuits, coffee or tea.

Running buffet

- Assortment of sandwiches, cocktail sausage rolls, bridge rolls, savouries, gherkins, cakes, tea and coffee.
- Chicken portions, assorted sandwiches and bridge rolls, sausage rolls, cocktail fancies, coffee and tea.
- Smoked salmon sandwiches, salads, savoury vol-au-vents, canapés, ham, beef and cheese sandwiches, cream pastries or fruit salad, coffee and tea.

The carvery

- Roast beef, turkey and ham carved from the bone, assortment of salads, potatoes, bridge rolls, fresh cream cakes, coffee, tea.
- Turkey, ham, roast beef, roast pork, ox tongue, smoked salmon, fresh salmon mayonnaise,

assorted salads, cream cakes and/or cheese and biscuits, coffee and tea.

Cocktail buffet

- Fresh salmon, smoked salmon, crab, pork, ham, ox tongue, cheese, egg, filled sandwiches and bridge rolls, savoury vol-au-vents, hot cocktail sausages and sausage rolls, toasted savouries and hot savoury snacks, prawns with dip.

Some caterers will arrange to serve food over several hours if the reception is to be a long one. For example, a reception buffet may be offered to the guests on arrival which could consist of canapés, snacks, vol-au-vents and bar snacks such as gherkins, stuffed olives, crisps and nuts.

A main meal may be served after a while when the guests have mixed and chatted and the bride and groom have had a chance to talk to many of their family and friends. This could be a cold meal such as fresh salmon with hollandaise sauce, new potatoes, and garden peas, rolls and butter, fruit and ice-cream, cheese and biscuits and coffee. As the evening goes on, especially if there is dancing, a selection of sandwiches, cakes and pastries plus tea and coffee may be offered.

These are all very traditional styles of menu and food, especially easy for outside catering firms to produce, deliver and serve in hired halls. Most hotels will offer similar menus as well as some more imaginative ones that require good cooking facilities on the premises. Restaurants used to producing and serving imaginative dishes every day will normally offer suggestions from their usual menus. There are also small caterers, often just a couple of cordon bleu trained cooks who can offer unusual and beautifully prepared and served meals. Always discuss the menu in great detail, offer your own ideas and suggestions if you have them, and get full quotations from everyone you talk to, making sure you know exactly what they offer and what is covered in the quotation.

Finding a caterer is similar to searching out a suitable hotel. Good restaurants may do outside catering; ask them and check in the local press and Yellow Pages. Ask for quotations and check what extras they can supply. Do they charge for hire of linen, crockery, glasses, flowers, cake stands, for example? Make sure they understand the facilities available in the hall or rooms you are hiring. Will they clear up afterwards? Check that VAT and service are included and whether tips are expected. Get everything in writing and confirm details. Make sure you understand exactly what you are getting and paying for.

The drinks

Alcohol, as everyone knows, is expensive, especially for large gatherings. It is not necessary to serve champagne throughout the entire reception, but it is expected for the toasts if alternative drinks are offered throughout the reception. A good sparkling wine could be drunk throughout, however.

It is usual to offer guests a drink on arrival, such as sherry (or red or white wine if only one type of drink is being offered during the reception). An open bar could be available serving wine, beer, cocktails, and/or spirits, and when this is the case it is now becoming more popular for the bar to be open and free to guests for a previously agreed length of time, after which they pay for the drinks themselves. This is certainly one way to cut down on heavy expenses at a large or long party.

Wine or a punch may be offered throughout the reception, with glasses of champagne brought in for the cake cutting, speeches and toasts.

It is always advisable to have a selection of non-alcoholic drinks available at a reception for children and adults who prefer not to drink alcohol. Light drinks such as spring water and apple juice are enjoyed, so is freshly squeezed orange juice. Also consider whether you will be serving Buck's Fizz (equal amounts of champagne or sparkling white wine and orange juice), a champagne cup, fruit punch, Pimms or Kir (white wine with a dash of cassis). Many people also like to drink beer, especially if there is dancing or a disco. Have some low-alcohol drinks available. And a cup of tea or coffee towards the end of the reception is always welcomed.

Some halls attached to churches do not allow alcohol to be served at all, in which case a little ingenuity is required to find suitable mixtures and non-alcoholic fruit punches to make the drinks at least look more exciting than plain orange squash. Investigate the no-alcohol wines, too.

Charges for drinks vary and must be discussed in advance with the caterers. Alcohol consumption can only be guessed and estimated so there is often a shortfall in the amount paid in advance and the final price to be paid. Make your arrangements in writing.

If you are organizing the wine, allow at least half a bottle of champagne per person if you are serving it throughout the reception but one bottle for six people should suffice if it is only served for the toasts. If sparkling wine is served throughout, allow half to three-quarters of a bottle per head. A choice of red, white or rosé wines may be offered – allow half to three-quarters of a bottle per person plus one bottle of sparkling wine or champagne for every six guests for the cake-cutting and toasts.

The cake

The wedding cake has a long tradition and history, but today a baker will offer a variety of styles and icing patterns. The size of the cake required will depend on the number of guests at the reception, how many pieces are to be boxed and sent to people unable to attend the celebration, and whether one layer will be kept for a future occasion such as a first anniversary party or for use as a christening cake for the first child. Every type of cake on offer can be scaled to serve the required number. As a rough guide, allow six to eight portions per pound of cake.

It is advisable to order the cake well before the wedding – six to eight weeks if possible. Although it is usual for a wedding cake to be a full fruit cake, any flavour can be ordered, including sponges and chocolate. Icing is traditionally white, but can be any colour. Cream is a popular choice and many brides choose a cake that is iced in a shade to match their dress, if they are not wearing white, or may choose a basically white-iced cake decorated with piping or icing rosettes in the same shade as the bridesmaids' dresses. Anyone who has a colour theme for their wedding would want the cake to echo it – pale blue, apricot, lemon and pale pink are favourites.

Cakes are usually square, round or heart-shaped, from one to four tiers but other more unusual shapes are also available. If the couple have a special interest in common the cake can be made to reflect this – in the shape of a racing car for example. The cake can be topped with a vase of flowers, exquisite icing sugar flowers moulded to match the flowers in the bride's bouquet, with figures of a bride and groom, or again if they have a joint interest, a decoration such as tennis racquets, skis, a boat or golf clubs can be used. Other alternatives include regimental badges, coats of arms, and personal monograms.

Most bakers make a charge or require a deposit on tier supports, cake boards or bases or any equipment they may supply such as a stand and knife. Cake top figures of the bride and groom and other decorations such as hearts, silver shoes, sprigs of flowers and so on can be bought from stationers and some florists. If the cake is being made as a present from a friend or family, many bakers will undertake to marzipan, ice and decorate the cake provided.

Wedding cakes are heavy but also fragile, and it is preferable to have the cake delivered direct to the reception. If the cake is damaged in transit it is then the bakery's responsibility to repair it and see that it is in perfect shape before it goes on show. Always ask the baker about ingredients and for a sample of the wedding cakes he bakes, as well as looking at his designs and ornaments for decoration. The cake is quite an expensive item, as well as an important one at the reception, so it is worth shopping around and getting exactly what you want.

The first slice of cake is cut by the bride and groom together – the bride's right hand on the knife handle, covered by her husband's right hand and the bride's left hand on top – which symbolizes their togetherness and the sharing of their future lives. The cake is then taken away to be cut and small slices are handed round to all the guests. If served on paper napkins, those guests who do not want to eat it immediately can carry it away easily.

If you do not want a cake (perhaps at the reception for a second marriage), consider a very special sweet – a tower of profiteroles for example, or something surrounded by spun sugar.

To keep tiers of fruit cake, wrap them in tissue paper and place in an airtight tin. The icing will discolour but some bakers will re-ice a cake they have made. Ask if this service is available when ordering.

A few extras

A nice addition, and part of wedding tradition, is the use of sugared almonds or bon bons handed to the guests from a basket by the small bridesmaids. Rice, confetti and rose petals are symbols of a happy and fertile marriage and can be showered on the bride and groom as they leave the reception for their honeymoon.

The music

Whether or not you have music at the reception depends on the type of celebration, the time of day and your budget. Discos or dances are often part of the celebration, but they need to be done properly and professionally. Background musak on an appalling sound system can be worse than no sound at all.

An evening sit-down meal of the formal kind may be followed by a dance, the music provided by a live band. If they are good they should be able to play a variety of types of music to keep all ages happy.

If the bride's parents would like a formal reception and the bride and groom would prefer something louder and livelier, both sets of wishes can be accommodated by having the formal reception after the wedding and a disco later that night. The bride can wear her wedding dress to the disco or change into an evening dress or something that reflects the informality of the setting. If friends invited to the disco have not been to the earlier reception, the bride and groom may like to have one tier of their wedding cake to cut for them, and although speeches are not required, someone is sure to want to say something to wish the couple a happy lifetime together! Food for the disco participants can be anything from Chinese to pizza to fish and chips or burgers – as informal as the couple desire. The first glasses of wine or beer may be provided but most people would expect to pay for their own drinks at an informal disco.

Whatever style of music you choose – and it could

range from a string quartet to a pop group, a harpist to a jazz band, a pianist to a dance band to a DJ with his selection of hit records – make sure you've seen and heard them in action before you book them, get quotations, and agree the hours they will play. As for everything else, get all agreements in writing.

Helpful services

In most big towns and cities there are companies which will organize all the wedding services, including the hire cars, flowers, photography, hiring a hall and catering for the reception, the cake, a disco, the printing of invitations, and other wedding stationery, video recordings of the wedding and even the rings, wedding clothes and presents for the bridal attendants. This takes away all the organization problems while still offering some choice – you make the decisions about what you want from what they have to offer and they do the work.

Alternatives

While many families want the more traditional types of reception described above, there are alternative ways to celebrate. Most popular among these is the disco, but other suggestions include American-style brunch, a champagne breakfast, a high tea, champagne and strawberries or a picnic in the country, and a late-night party. Londoners have the opportunity to hire one of the many pleasure boats that operate on the Thames. Catering, bar service and music are all taken care of and the Thames by night (in good weather!) is beautiful. Many West End theatres allow receptions in special rooms or the crush bar. With more couples choosing to pay for their own receptions they feel more free to celebrate in their own style – and enjoy a party rather than a somewhat formal and at times impersonal reception. The important thing is that you celebrate in the way you like best.

25

Wedding Presents

As soon as people know you are getting married – and especially when they receive an invitation for the wedding – they will want to know what to buy for a wedding present. There has been much controversy about the 'blatant' sending out of a gift list with the invitation, and indeed on the subject of even compiling one, but for brides as well as sensible relatives and friends, a carefully compiled and thought-out wedding present list is essential.

The list can be one taken from a bridal magazine or compiled at home. It should list the product required as well as details such as make, style or design, name or number, colour, number required and a column at the end big enough to write in the name or initials of the giver. An extra column can be added on the master list to tick off whether a thank-you letter has been written. If you are a bit slow about writing letters, jog your memory by putting down the date the present was received – thank yous should be prompt.

Having a list avoids the otherwise inevitable receipt of several versions of the same product. No one needs five salt and pepper sets or even two washing machines! Include a good selection of inexpensive as well as medium-priced and expensive items.

If a rather expensive dinner service is what you've set your heart on, remember that several relatives or friends can all band together to provide this – suggest that some buy the cups and saucers, others buy dinner plates, someone else buys the coffee pot, and so on, until you have built up the complete set. This could become a joint family venture if there are many members of the same family coming to the wedding. (List some cheaper china for everyday use, too.) When building up a set in this way, where items can be bought separately, consider your actual needs. You may need eight settings for dinner at one time but as there is less likely to be eight for breakfast you may only need four egg cups. Expensive cutlery can be bought in the same way – three or four friends buying two place settings each. Again, you could list some cheap cutlery for everyday use.

Many people hand over the organizing of the gift list to one of the big stores offering a bride's list service. The bride and groom go along to the chosen store and together choose everything they will need for their new home. Some shops employ a special advisor to help. Once all the details are completed, the shop keeps the list and wedding guests can consult it to see what has already been bought and promised. Most shops will allow guests to order by post or telephone, and may offer a gift-wrapping service and special card for the giver to add a message and sign.

Should you decide to have a store arrange your wedding list, check on the services they offer. The more personal the better – a good salesperson can often discreetly persuade a guest to buy something you really need, even if it is considered mundane, or to buy part of an expensive item, such as a dinner plate or a place setting from a canteen of cutlery. What sort of delivery service do they offer? If they dispatch something every time a purchase is made, someone has to stay home and wait for it! And you don't want gifts arriving the day after the wedding. Is the delivery service free? Is the shop computerized and will they keep you updated on what has been bought and by whom? How often? Do they accept telephone and credit card orders? Do they offer a gift-wrap service, and is it free? Will they exchange duplicated gifts that have not been bought from the store originally?

Some shops deduct say five per cent from all presents bought from the list and allow the bride and groom that money against incomplete sets of china or cutlery, for example; others offer a gift voucher worth five or ten per cent of the total amount spent on the list. Remember it isn't essential to have your wedding list at a local store. With telephone ordering and computerized lists, all your guests need to do is lift the telephone.

If you know the colour schemes for your new home it will be very helpful – sheets, bed linen, towels, bathroom fixtures, kitchen equipment and so on can all be co-ordinated, and will look much more attractive than a hotch-potch of assorted colours and designs.

With such a wide range of products available and so much choice, it is especially important to take much care and time when compiling a gift list. Bear in mind that you will have to live with the consequences of your choice perhaps for many years – a strong design in vibrant colours can be fun for a while but when seen in a complete set of china, day after day, it can be overwhelming. Simple design in white or basic colours or with a small pattern is easier to live with, and good design never 'dates'.

Your mother will be very involved in the receiving of the gifts if you are living at home or if the presents are being sent to your parents' home. But don't forget your future mother-in-law amid all the excitement. Keep in touch with her, ask her to go shopping with you, phone her when a present arrives from her family or friends. She will enjoy feeling involved in the wedding preparations and be pleased to share in the planning – this could be the basis for a good future relationship with her.

The following lists contain ideas to help you decide on suitable wedding presents to put on your list.

Kitchen

Baking tins
Bread bin
Bread board
Bread knife
Carving dish and knife
Casserole set
Corkscrew
Dishwasher
Electric kettle
Frying pan

Coffee grinder
Coffee percolator
Cooker
Cookery books
Microwave oven
Infra-red grill
Carpet shampooer
Carpet sweeper
Deep freeze
Dustbin

Deep fat fryer
Saucepans
Slo-cooker
Misc. kitchen furniture
Kitchen knives
Kitchen scales
Knife sharpener
Mixer and accessories
Liquidizer
Mixing bowls
Pyrex dishes
Oven gloves
Oven-to-table ware
Pressure cooker
Refrigerator
Rolling pin
Pastry board
Salad bowl and servers
Sieve
Spice rack
Storage jars/tins
Tea towels
Toaster
Trays
Vegetable rack
Brushes/brush set
Air extractor fan
Cooker hood
Double boiler
Hostess trolley
Kitchen scissors
Nut crackers
Vacuum flask

Pedal bin
Spin/tumble dryer
Washing machine
Stepladder
Colander
Barbecue
Fondu set
Garlic press
Omelette pan
Rotisserie/spit
Tea caddy
Vacuum ice bucket
Wine rack
Toast rack
Floor polisher
Iron
Ironing board
Washing line
Can opener
Cutlery set
Chopping boards
Timer
Plate drainer
Sink set
Toasted sandwich maker
Food processor
Towel holder
Cheese grater
Herb mouli
Juice extractor
Measuring cups and
     spoons
Spatula

Wood spoons
Dusters

Whisk
Wok

Miscellaneous

Garden furniture
Garden tools
Power mower
Carpets/rugs
Lamps
Ornaments
Mirrors
Luggage
Wastepaper bins
Ash trays
Books
Cigarette box
Picnic basket
Window accessories
Shrubs & trees

Radio
Needlework basket
Cassette recorder
Car rug
Camera
Drink/Wine
Calculator
Vacuum cleaner
Pictures
Projector
Typewriter
Sewing machine
Tool kit
Wheelbarrow
Electric drill

Bedroom

Bed
Bedspread
Duvet
Blankets
Electric blanket
Eiderdown
Pillows
Mattress covers

Pillowcases
Duvet covers
Sheets
Rugs
Tea maker
Clock/radio
Lamps
Portable television

Dining room

Trolley
Breakfast service
Dinner service
Tea service
Place settings
Soup tureen
Vegetable dishes
Soup dishes
Serving spoons and forks
Canteen of cutlery
Jam pot and spoon
Pepper & salt mills
Carafe
Wine glasses
Brandy goblets
Beer glasses
Whisky glasses
Tumblers
Water jug set
Vases
Fruit bowls
Cutlery set
Condiment set
Butter knives
Cake server
Fish server
Steak knives and forks
Champagne glasses
Liqueur glasses
Sherry glasses

Coffee set
Coffee pot
Tea pot
Butter dish
Dessert dish
Egg cups
Mugs
Place mats
Sugar bowl
Sugar tongs
Coasters
Cake knives & forks
Fish knives & forks
Candle sticks
Cheeseboard & knife
Cream jug
Tea strainer
Table cloths
Serviettes
Gravy boat
Table & chairs
Sideboard
Plate warmer
Sauce boat
Coffee spoons
Grapefruit knife
Grapefruit spoons
Sugar sifter
Teaspoons
Decanter
Cocktail glasses

Living room

TV	Chairs
Magazine rack	Coffee tables
Carpet	Clocks
Cushions	Radio
Settee	Stereo
Video	CD player

Bathroom

First aid kit	Drying rack
Bath mat	Mirror
Bathroom scales	Shower curtain
Bath towels	Soap holder
Hand towels	Toothbrush holder
Linen basket	Guest towels
Bathroom cabinet	Large bathsheets
Shower fitting	Tissue holder

Displaying the gifts

Some families like to have a display of the wedding gifts, either at the bride's parents' home or at the reception. Presents of the same type are placed together – kitchen things, linen, china – but don't put duplicates side by side. One place setting of china, glass or cutlery is sufficient.

Do you use cards to indicate who sent what? It saves the inevitable questioning but not having them saves comments and comparisons. The choice is yours. The choice is also yours as to whether you display cheques to show the amount or whether you arrange them so only the signatures show – or whether you write a card stating 'Cheque from Aunty Doris'.

Exchanging gifts

A thorny problem, this, and one that has to be decided on merit. If the sender is someone you know well you could explain that you have received two identical presents and would like to exchange one. Only do that if you are sure the person is unlikely to be hurt by the request. If the unwanted gift was sent by someone far away or who is unlikely to visit, it may be safe to quietly exchange it for something you like better. Rather than risk offending or hurting someone it is often better to keep the original present.

What if . . .?

If you already have a home, you will know exactly what you need and want. Make up a list and send a copy to anyone who asks. It may include a specific design of china or glass that you are collecting, a picture you love, suggestions for records, videos or CDs, a telephone answering machine, a mini or portable television, a subscription to your favourite magazine, life membership of an organization you'd like to belong to, a tree or plants for the garden, wine, jewellery, even tickets to an opera or show you want to see as a treat.

Received with thanks

Once you begin to receive wedding presents you will want to send thank-you notes. It is best to write them as you receive the gifts – many a bride has come back from honeymoon to face the thought of having umpteen letters to write at the same time as trying to get her new home organized. That can be a daunting prospect. Do a few every day so they don't pile up.

Make sure you keep a record of every gift and a note of who sent it. It's a good idea to make a column alongside the wedding guest list in which you can note the presents received.

Traditionally, when a present is sent by a couple the thank-you note is only addressed to the wife (like the wedding invitation), but her husband should be mentioned in the note, e.g. 'How kind of you and Jack to send us. . . .' However, if you feel like flouting that convention, why not? After all the gift came from the couple!

If the gift comes from a group of people, say from office or workmates, you can write to them collectively but address the note to the 'head' person or the one you know best. If two or three friends send a joint present each of them should receive a personal thank-you card.

Make each note sincere and grateful. Although the letter may be brief it should be interesting. Mention the gift specifically, say how useful it will be. For distant relatives or friends you don't see often, take time to write a little more. Tell them of your wedding plans, your new home – and expand and make it a really warm note. Don't forget to mention your spouse's name in the letter.

When thanking someone for a cheque it is not considered etiquette to mention the actual amount. Write about what you have bought or how you plan to use their generous gift.

Notes should be signed 'affectionately', 'sincerely', 'with love' as the case may be, depending on your relationship with the people who have sent the gift. If you don't know the person well, include your surname as well as given name.

In the case of duplicate gifts, write each thank-you note as though it was the only one received. And if you don't know what the item is, there are many ways of tactfully thanking the sender without giving away your bewilderment.

There are so many varieties of pretty stationery available in the shops that it will not be difficult to find something suitable for thank-you notes. You can also buy special cards which have 'Thank you for your wedding gift' inscribed on the outside with the inside left blank for your own message of thanks – but do include a chatty message, or the recipient may feel you don't care very much.

Repeating the same kind of message so many times can become tedious, but as you'll make someone just as happy with the note you send as they made you with the gift, it is worth taking time and consideration in writing the thank-you letter. It is also a good reason for writing and sending off the card or letter as soon as the present is received. There is an old adage that says 'it is better to give than receive', so making a special effort with a thank-you note may give much more joy than you ever imagined.

26

On the Day: Some Thoughts for the Bride

It's the bride's special day – as everyone keeps reminding you – but even for the bride there are certain duties and rules of etiquette.

Before you say good-bye to the bridesmaids, as they leave for the church with your mother, you can present them with their gift from you and your groom, especially if it is jewellery as they will want to wear it at the ceremony. (However, if it is bulky it would be better to give it to them at a 'hen party' or 'bridesmaids' lunch' a day or two before the wedding.)

Try to arrange things so you have a few minutes alone with your father before he accompanies you to the altar. It will probably be the last chance for a quiet chat together, and you will want to thank him for everything.

Another small thank-you that will be appreciated is to leave a note and present by your parents' bed, for them to find when they get home. It need only be a small gesture, but it will be appreciated in a big way.

Before you leave for the church have a last-minute

check – are you wearing something old, something new, something borrowed and something blue? Most brides like to keep that tradition going. Is your engagement ring on your right hand?

At the church you take your father's right arm and, followed by your bridesmaids, walk up the aisle where you meet your groom and stand on his left. He'll appreciate a warm smile! Your chief bridesmaid will take your bouquet before you exchange rings. On conclusion of the actual ceremony you sign the register and receive the 'marriage lines' which belong to you. This will be the last time you will officially sign in your maiden name – unless you have decided to carry on using it after you are married.

As you will arrive first at the reception take this opportunity to use the nearest ladies room and freshen up. Your mother will probably keep some lipstick, powder and small perfume spray in her handbag for you for just this moment.

As the guests arrive, it is your duty to greet them all individually. Don't spend too much time gossiping or you'll hold up the line – you can talk to them later.

After the meal or buffet, you and your husband will cut the cake. Place your right hand on the knife, the groom places his right hand over yours, and your left hand goes on top of that. It is an American tradition for the first piece of cake to be halved, and for the bride to offer one piece to the groom and the groom to offer the other piece to his bride. That is a tradition you may like to copy for it is full of the symbolism of sharing, which is what marriage is all about.

If there is a dance or party afterwards it is customary for you and your husband to begin the dancing and then to part to bring your parents on to the floor. Once all the close family are on the dance floor, everyone else can join in.

Now you can do the rounds of all your guests. Try to talk to everyone, at least briefly, but they will understand if you don't spend too long in their company. You can always compensate by inviting people to dinner later in your new home.

This is the stage to watch your alcohol consumption. The blushing bride may become a little too flushed. It's fun to have a few drinks, but if you drink too much your wedding night could be spent in the bathroom rather than the bedroom.

Once you've changed for your honeymoon trip it's time to return to the party and say your good-byes. Be prepared for the traditional fun and games of a decorated car – but take the decorations off as soon as you get round the corner. They are a hazard for driving.

Another tradition is to throw your bouquet for one of the bridesmaids to catch. You may like to preserve a few flowers from the bouquet, or present it to a grandmother, or place it on the grave of a close relative. What you do with the bouquet is entirely up to you. If the flowers are made of silk you will probably want to keep it.

Now all you have to do is enjoy your honeymoon, relax a bit, and look forward to your new status of Mr and Mrs.

27

The Perfect Wedding Guest

You've been invited to a wedding – what is expected of you as a guest? Before the wedding you will want to send a present to the couple, something of the bride's choice. You can ask her what she would like to receive but she is likely to have a gift list or tell you at which store she has registered her wedding present list. If you accept a wedding invitation, the convention is that you send a gift. If you do not attend the ceremony or reception it is a personal choice as to whether or not you send a gift – but most people do, especially when it concerns a close friend or member of the family.

Arrive at the church or register office in good time. The time stated on the invitation card is the time the ceremony is due to begin. It is customary to arrive about ten minutes early. If the church or register office is small and you are invited only to the reception, get there on time to make sure you will be able to toast the bride and groom before they leave if they are going on honeymoon from the reception.

At a formal white wedding in church, the ushers will meet you at the door and guide you to a pew, asking whether you are a relative or friend of the bride or groom. If not directed, guests may sit where they wish, remembering that the front pews are reserved for family on both sides.

Before the service begins, guests tend to be friendly but rather muted, remembering the solemnity of the occasion within the church building. You can nod and smile and chat briefly and quietly – but leave the noise and gossip for afterwards.

Many guests will be unfamiliar with the church, religion or service that takes place. This alone is a subduing experience and the only thing to do is sit quietly and follow everyone else.

When the religious ceremony is over and the bridal entourage walks down the aisle, the social part of the day can begin. Everyone smiles at the bride as she leaves the church. The family, the people in the front pews, leave the church first and are followed by the other guests.

Outside the church, the guests stay around while the professional photographs are taken and can take some photographs themselves. Check beforehand whether the throwing of confetti is acceptable or not. Once the bride and groom have left for the reception, followed by the bridesmaids and close family, the remaining guests can also leave for the reception.

At the reception there is usually a receiving line. At a very formal wedding there may be a major-domo. In this case, give your name to be announced. Otherwise simply stand in line, join the queue and shake hands when it's your turn. It is all a formality, so don't hold up the line by stopping for a chat: that can come later. A quick handshake – or kiss if you know the people very well – a brief remark and then move on.

After you have moved on from the receiving line you will probably be offered a celebratory drink and you can mix and chat to other guests. At a buffet reception, you may be asked to help yourself to food from a long table, or at a cocktail party style reception the food and drink is likely to be brought round on trays and offered to you.

At a formal reception with a sit-down meal, places are usually marked with the guests' names. If a dance is held afterwards, the bride and groom take the floor first, then their parents. Eventually everyone can join in the dancing.

As there is seldom anyone to introduce guests to each other, it's up to you to circulate and introduce yourself. As everyone is there to celebrate the same occasion it is very easy to communicate by simply introducing yourself by name and saying 'Mary and I were at school together', or 'I'm the groom's brother-in-law' or whatever the relationship or connection is.

When the bride and groom leave the reception party for their honeymoon, the party usually begins to break up. You are now expected to seek out the bride's mother and thank her, having a brief chat about how pretty her daughter looked and how you hope the couple will be very happy.

28

The Bride's Parents

The bride's mother traditionally stage-manages the show, the bride's father (traditionally) pays. Today, when the bride's mother is as likely as the bride to be working, they often share the planning and work between them. Essentially, she has to gather all her organizing abilities to full strength – and be tactful and diplomatic!

Let's look at the conventional plan of action for the bride's mother: deciding, together with her daughter, on the size of the guest list and who should be invited; liaising with the groom's parents on their invitation list; sending out the invitations and keeping a list of acceptances and refusals; keeping the groom's family informed; arranging press announcements; keeping the wedding present list and storing the gifts; choosing the flowers for the wedding and reception decorations; helping the bride choose her bouquet and to choose the photographer, car hire firm and so on; planning and organizing the reception; planning her own dress and consulting other central members of the wedding party as to colour scheming. The bride may also welcome some help when choosing her dress.

On the day of the wedding, as well as getting

herself ready for the important occasion, the bride's mum will be happy to help her daughter dress if she is leaving from the family home. The bride's mother should leave the house before her daughter, perhaps with the bridesmaids or with a close friend or a family member. When she arrives at the church, she will be escorted to her seat by an usher, but will be the last person to take her seat. If there are no attendants to do so, she will look after the bride's bouquet, carrying it with her during the procession to the signing of the register.

At the reception, as hostess the bride's mother is a central character – she will be the first person to be greeted in the receiving line, and will be thanked in the speeches. She will also be a 'real mum' if she carries a small make-up repair kit in her handbag in case the bride wants to freshen up before the photographs or before the guests arrive at the reception.

The bride's father tends to be a forgotten character, the bride and her mother being centre-stage but, after the groom, he is the most important man of the day. It is a significant day for him, too. He is giving her away. With the bride, he is the last person to leave for the church. He helps her arrange her dress in the car – and holds her hand. He walks up the aisle with his daughter on his right arm and stands on her left at the chancel steps. He goes to his seat in the front pew when he has given her away.

Today the bride's father is likely to have much more say in the planning and organizing of his daughter's wedding than he would have done a few years ago – and probably feels secretly pleased about that. He is expected to give emotional and practical support to his daughter to keep her as calm and relaxed as possible while escorting her to the ceremony and up the aisle. At a civil ceremony he may take her to the register office.

When it comes to organizing the wedding, the bride's best friend could well be her mother; in being supportive, caring and helpful – her father.

29
The Groom's Parents

The bride's parents tend to get the most involved in the wedding preparations and the groom's parents often feel they haven't a role. You have! You are special guests of honour at the wedding and can certainly take an interest in the preparations and activities leading up to the ceremony.

If you do not know the bride-to-be, remedy that as soon as possible. If you do, and your son tells you the news of their engagement, telephone her immediately and express your happiness.

If you have not yet met the bride's parents, get your son to arrange a meeting for you all. Invite them to your home. If they live a distance away, write to them and introduce yourselves, saying that you hope to meet them before the wedding.

Traditional financial arrangements for the wedding are changing (see pp 43–44), and you may wish to make a contribution to the costs of the reception. Discuss this with the bride's parents. If they do not want to split costs, you may be able to help the bride and groom directly by giving them a cheque or helping to buy furniture for their new home. It is a nice gesture to give the bride a personal present, perhaps a piece of jewellery.

Be as co-operative as you can to the bride and her family – but don't try to take over! If the bride's parents are paying all the bills, be as helpful as you can in providing a guest list to suit their needs and pocket, and give them the names of your guests as early as possible after they have been requested. You can offer to address some of the envelopes, though the bride's family may want to do this.

When it comes to what to wear, the bride's family may have decided on styles and colour scheming to create a complete picture. The bride's mother selects her outfit first. The groom's father should dress in the same type of suit as the other men in the party – morning dress, dark business suit or lounge suit.

If there is to be a rehearsal just before the wedding, you may like to hold a small party or have a meal in a restaurant (or even just a drink) with the participants. The groom's father can then give a toast to the bride.

At the church the head/chief usher will escort you to your pew. The groom's father follows a few steps behind his wife as she is shown to the pew – which is the first pew on the right-hand side of the church. The groom's father sits in the aisle seat.

You will leave the church at the recessional, the groom's father being paired with the bride's mother and the groom's mother with the bride's father. This indicates the uniting of the two families.

When all the photographs have been taken you will be among the first to leave for the reception and if there is to be a receiving line will take your place in the line to greet guests.

Seating arrangements will be made for the reception if there is to be a sit-down meal, with place cards on the top table.

When the bride and groom leave on honeymoon, give them a big hug and your wishes for their happiness.

30

When Parents are Divorced

Weddings are family happenings and should be happy. When a marriage has broken up there can be antagonisms that don't mend easily, but the most important thing for divorced parents to do is to conceal their personal feelings and resolve to forget their differences on their daughter's or son's wedding day. The situation can be handled with dignity, calm and co-operation.

Invitations are usually sent out by the parent with whom the bride lives, or lived until she left home. See the chapter on wedding invitations for correct wording. Americans solve the problem by issuing two lots of invitations, one to the ceremony and another to the reception, with the mother's (and her new husband's) name as host and hostess at the reception. This is not usually followed here because wedding invitations, in British custom, are combined ceremony/reception invitations.

The divorced parents of the bride and groom play a major role at the wedding and their new partners take a back seat, appearing simply as guests, albeit distinguished guests. This can be uncomfortable but must be handled with acceptance – it's the bride and groom's day. If the parents are separated but not divorced they should ignore their separation and issue invitations as a married couple.

Church seating arrangements are as follows: the mother of the bride sits in the first pew on the left of the church. If she has not remarried she can sit alone or invite a close relative to sit with her. The head usher can be her escort as the bridal party leaves the church. After giving the bride away, her father sits in the second or third pew on the left with his parents or with his wife if she attends. The same seating arrangements apply to the groom's parents if they are divorced.

If there is to be a receiving line at the reception, the people who have arranged the reception should stand in the line. This is usually the bride's mother and father, and their new partners are not part of the receiving line.

Family squabbles should not be allowed to interfere with this special day, and if everyone is determined that they won't – they won't!

31

Making a Speech

Being expected to make a speech is often the part of the wedding celebration that causes the most worry – at least for the people concerned. But a little bit of serious thought beforehand plus good preparation and some practising is all that's needed to dispel most fears.

Even experienced public speakers will admit to being a little nervous, but they have learned that self-confidence comes from being comfortable with the words they are going to say and with the feeling of acceptance of themselves by their audience. As a wedding is a family affair and everyone is happy, a speaker at a wedding knows he has his audience on his side (even if there are a few friendly jokes and interruptions). Being comfortable with the words that are going to be said means plenty of preparation for the speech beforehand – collecting ideas and material, writing it out, pruning it and editing it until the speech is short yet contains much of what you want to say.

So 'preparation' is a key word in the plan. As soon as you have been asked to make a short speech and/or offer a toast, start thinking about what you will say. The best received 'few words' are the ones tailored to a specific occasion, so it is not ideal to rush off to the nearest book on the subject and copy out a prepared speech.

You do not have to write the whole speech from beginning to end in one go – in fact that is not a good idea at all. Keep a small notebook handy so you can jot down ideas for the speech as they come to you. With plenty of time to plan, you can relax your mind and the ideas will come – an interesting incident from the bride's childhood, for example, or an odd nice thought of your own about marriage and happiness. The important thing at this stage is to put the thought down on paper – a simple sentence or just one word to jog your memory will do. It is not necessary to worry about the correct grammar or the most suitable adjective. That comes later when the speech starts taking shape.

Apt quotations, anecdotes and jokes (not blue) can be used in a speech for a wedding, but not too many. Remember the purpose or aim of the speech you are to give as well as the audience who are going to receive it. A wedding is not the time to offer jokes that could upset some members of the family or friends. It should go without saying that you remember names and get them right! And keep to the point! When you stand up to propose a toast and 'say a few words' don't forget your aim – to propose a toast. There have been many people before you who have got carried away by their own rhetoric and have had to be reminded to toast the bride and groom!

After a time your notebook will contain plenty of ideas and suggestions. Go through them carefully, choose the ones you want to use and ruthlessly reject the others. Ask yourself the question: 'What would they like to hear?' Don't incorporate too many ideas in your speech, you will only confuse the listeners, or make the speech too long.

At school you were probably taught that a story should have a beginning, a middle and an end. It is much the same with a good speech, which should flow easily from topic to topic within this framework. The introduction needs something to gain the guests' attention and make them feel involved. Many of the speeches and toasts made at a wedding reception are really representing the good wishes of the whole community. This is especially true of the one given by the bride's father, uncle or close friend of the family. A story or joke which they can all relate to makes a good introduction.

Having gained the attention of your audience you can lead into the body of the speech. The aim of a wedding speech is to entertain, but keep it light and preferably unembarrassing. Think of the words you use as a conversation with the guests at the reception – talk *with* people, not at them.

Words in their written and spoken form are experienced differently by their receiver. If the reader is presented with a long sentence, he or she can always go back over it if it has not been understood or taken in; there is no such way to catch up with the spoken word. So keep your sentences as short as possible. Only use words you are sure you know the meaning of – everyone has a joke at the expense of someone who used words in the wrong context.

Jokes can come into a speech at a wedding recep-

tion – indeed they are often expected – but avoid
blue, risqué, sick or religious ones. Stag night jokes
are not ones to use at the wedding day celebration;
one line often used by a best man during his speech
and one which always gets a laugh is simply 'None
of the jokes I tried out last night at the party seem
too suitable for today.'

A good motto to remember is: try to leave your
audience feeling they want to hear more from you
rather than that they've heard plenty already. The
conclusion of the speech is important. It should
neatly tie up the earlier part and lead easily and
naturally into the toast.

Once you feel you have gathered together what
you wish to say, and have edited it carefully, have a
rehearsal. You will be the centre of attention for the
few minutes that you will be addressing the gather-
ing, so make sure you make the best of the time –
both in what you say and how you say it. Practise
in front of a mirror, in an empty room. Stand up
straight with feet apart so you feel comfortable and
do not shuffle or sway around. Speak a little more
slowly and deliberately than normal. A voice pitched
in the middle range and a little louder than usual
should carry around most reception halls. There is
no need to shout – that is irritating for the listeners.
A tape recorder will not necessarily give you an exact
reproduction of your tone of voice but can be useful
for practising and rehearsal purposes to help with
timing, intonation and punctuation. It will give you
some idea of how you will sound to an audience. The
mirror will show you how you are likely to appear to
the guests – overdoing gestures, for example, can be

distracting. If you do not feel comfortable with what you have to say, think again, and possibly do some re-writing until you are happy.

With all the time spent writing and rehearsing, much of the speech will be in your mind and should be easy to remember. The extremes of reading a speech directly from a piece of paper or learning it precisely and repeating it verbatim from memory should be avoided. Remember what you can. You may remember it all quite easily, but it is always safer to take with you a few brief notes as reminders, just in case you need a prompt. A small card or two, held in the palm of your hand, can contain just a word or short sentence to remind you of the anecdote or joke and the order of subject matter of the speech. This will act as a 'memory jogger' and make you feel a little more secure.

When delivering the speech or proposing the toast, don't try to put on an accent that isn't your normal one. Stick to your own pronunciation. If you are not happy with your own accent, don't try to put on a so-called 'cultured' voice. It just sounds insincere and pretentious and will not be welcomed by listeners.

Most speeches for social occasions should last at the most five minutes, and this goes for wedding speeches, too. Prepare a maximum of four minutes – there's sure to be some laughter or even applause which will add a minute or more. Remember there are other people to follow you, or if you are the last speaker remember that the guests will have heard others and be wanting to get on with celebrating. The best motto of all about wedding speeches is: *keep it short!*

To propose the health of the bride and groom, ask everyone to raise their glasses to the happiness of 'the bride and groom' or more informally, 'Janet and John'.

Here is a round-up of basic principles and a few tips for speechmakers:

- Think carefully about what you want to say and thoroughly prepare the speech.
- Avoid any joke that may embarrass. Remember your audience will consist of a wide age range with people of differing backgrounds and sensibilities.
- Use simple words and avoid 'clever' phraseology.
- There is no need to attempt to memorize a speech word for word. You will be concentrating on remembering the next word instead of being aware of delivery.
- Keep a few notes that can be referred to unobtrusively.
- Look at the audience, address or 'converse' with them.
- Don't speak too quickly or keep your head down.
- Try to smile naturally without using a forced grin.
- Use your own accent and normal voice.
- Rehearse your speech in front of a mirror, preferably wearing the clothes you plan to be wearing at the reception.
- A tape recorder can be helpful.
- If you want to try out your speech on a listener before you deliver it at the reception, choose just one person whose judgement you trust.
- Keep the speech short but effective.

- Go to the loo in good time before the speeches start!
- Leave the serious drinking until after you've made the speech – a drunken toast and speech is embarrassing for all and is neither appreciated nor funny.
- Have a glass of water handy, just in case you get a throat tickle.
- Have confidence.

These hints on speech preparation and delivery are intended to be of help to everyone who has to 'say a few words' at a wedding, but some couples (and families) will want more time spent on the speeches than others. The style, formality or informality of the wedding will often dictate the speech requirements. With tradition playing such a big part at weddings it is almost expected that some of the 'old chestnuts' of wedding speeches are trotted out.

A simple toast to the bride and groom, delivered by the father of the bride, or a godparent, uncle or family friend will be on the lines of 'I propose the health of Mary and John – to the bride and groom – may they live happily ever after'. If this is preceded by 'I fell in love with Mary twenty years ago when I first saw her as a tiny baby in her pram – she's grown a lot since then, taller and even prettier – and John's a lucky man . . .' or 'when I saw Mary in her christening robes I never thought I'd be lucky enough to be here to propose this toast all these years later' or even 'May all their troubles be little ones', no one is going to complain. Weddings are a time for expressing sentiments.

The bridegroom replies by thanking the first speaker and practically everyone in sight – particularly the bride's parents for producing their daughter, for a wonderful wedding reception, for accepting him and being kind to his friends and to all the guests for being with them and sharing their happiness and, of course, for their presents. He could mention some guests by name – for instance, anyone who has travelled a particularly long distance to be at the wedding, and he should also thank his own parents, saying how much he has appreciated their loving support throughout his life. His speech need not be long and can be kept in the 'I know I'm a lucky man' vein. He needn't tell any jokes, though the well-worn ones seem to creep in, like 'I was told to stand up, speak up and shut up', and 'I'd like to thank whoever gave me the rolling pin'. Many a groom has got by with 'Mary and I want to thank you all and we both know that with such good friends around us our life together will be happy.' At the end of his speech, the bridegroom should propose a toast to the bridesmaids (and pageboys if there are any).

The best man, in reply, can say something (good) about the groom and express his delight at being expected to kiss the bridesmaids. If he introduced the couple he can express his sorrow at being the best man when he'd hoped to be the bridegroom. If Telemessages have been received he may read some or all of them – depending on content! This is something that should be decided and agreed upon beforehand, both to avoid potential embarrassment and, if there are a lot, to avoid tedious repetition of very similar messages from people who may not be known by other guests. (Telemessages could always be handed round afterwards so anyone who wants to read them can do so – or pinned up on a board in a convenient location.) Finally, the best man can propose a toast to the bride.

The bride by tradition is not expected to make a speech – but traditions can be broken!

32

Thank-you Presents

It is customary for the bride and groom to say 'thank you' to their attendants at the wedding by giving them a small gift as a memento of the occasion. It is often difficult to know what to choose, so here are a few ideas.

A small bridesmaid, flower girl or page could be given their first watch, transistor radio, calculator or simple camera. An inexpensive camera is also a good choice for a teenager – give it fully loaded with film for use after the wedding ceremony. A gift of jewellery is traditional for bridesmaids of any age – a silver ingot stamped with the year of the wedding would be a permanent reminder (and could gain in value). Earrings, a pretty bracelet or charm or locket on a chain could be worn at the ceremony as could a piece of jewellery containing the bridesmaid's birthstone or a stone of the colour of her dress. A simple chain hung with the bridesmaid's initial or name would be a welcome gift, as would an identity bracelet or silver bracelet with heart-shaped links. A young bridesmaid could be given a silver bracelet with a couple of charms attached, with additional charms given as gifts on future birthdays.

An adult bridesmaid or matron of honour may be

a collector of, say, fine china, glass or ornaments, in which case she would appreciate a specially chosen item for her collection. Children are great collectors so an autograph album could be a good choice, or a new board game, a birthday book, a classic children's book or framed picture. Attractively bound bridesmaids' bibles and prayer books, similar to, but smaller than the bride's, are available, and could be carried at the wedding. As a special memento, have a dried flower arrangement (using the type of flowers to be carried in the posies or bouquets) mounted and framed.

For the best man, cufflinks are often a good choice or an engraved writing set or fountain pen. A personalized gift set could be given to the best man with each of the ushers receiving a pen engraved with their initials. A pewter tankard, personally engraved with the recipient's initials and the date of the wedding would be a gift long remembered, as would an engraved lighter. Many gifts can be personalized by engraving; not only metals but glass, too, and wine goblets are often favoured for each of the adult attendants, male and female.

Other ideas for presents include: wall hangings of various kinds including framed prints or pictures, wood carvings, an engraved vase, a silver photograph frame, an evening bag, a beauty case, hand luggage or a leather purse, an attractive piece of china or miniature, an embroidered shawl, a chess set, an executive desk-top toy or a well-produced art book.

A thought that will be much appreciated is a thank-you gift for parents, perhaps left beside their bed just before the bride and her father leave for the church.

It does not have to be a large present – it's a case of 'the thought that counts'.

If, after the wedding, you find you have a favourite wedding photograph that you would like to give to special friends, close family or people who have been particularly kind or helpful, have some prints made and mounted attractively and send them one, suitably inscribed with your thanks or special thoughts.

33

Changing Your Name

Most women take their husband's name on marriage
– but not all. It is not a legal necessity to do so
but it is a long-held tradition and is often socially
expected.

A problem arises for women who are known in
their business and professional lives by their maiden
name and for whom to change it could cause diffi--
culties. They tend to lead a schizophrenic existence
with one name for work and another for the bank
and at the dry cleaners. Sometimes, they admit, they
get confused, but continue to use two names. One
solution frequently used in America is to combine
husband and wife's surname into a double-barrelled
name.

When you get married there are certain govern-
ment departments who will want to know about it –
HM Inspector of Taxes, (who will also want to know
whether you wish to be taxed jointly or separately),
National Insurance and Social Security (if relevant)
and the National Health Service are the most
important.

Your bank will want to know and will change the
name on your cheques and cheque guarantee card.
They will also want new specimen signatures from

you. And will you have a joint account or separate accounts or both? Tell the building society, post office or any organization with whom you have a savings account.

If you have any shares or insurance policies, inform the company about your change of name and address (if applicable). You may want to change the name of beneficiaries on the life assurance policy, as may your groom. Remind him – or at least talk about the subject. The same goes for wills.

Other change of name advices include your employer, of course, and all credit card companies, who will issue you with new cards; and you may wish to have your passport in your married name. If you own a car, the registration document should be changed to your new name, and so should your driving licence.

It is a good idea to have a medical and dental check-up before the wedding, so tell your doctor and dentist they will be seeing the same patient in future, but under a different name.

34

Contraception – A Simple Guide

Few newlyweds today want to start a family immediately; nor do they want to do as their grandparents did and have plenty of unplanned babies. So before the wedding day it is best to get advice on the most suitable form of contraception for you both, and it is very important that this should be discussed between you. You both need to know the other's views on whether you want to have children and to share the responsibility and decisions on birth control. The address of the local family planning clinic is in the telephone directory if you do not want to discuss contraception with the family doctor. The following is a brief look at the types of contraception available, how they work, their advantages and disadvantages.

The pill is one of the most popular methods of birth control in Britain and around the world. There are two types, the combined oestrogen and progestrogen pill in which chemicals similar to natural hormones prevent ovulation in the woman, and the progestogen only ('mini-pill') which works (and is taken) in a different way. With the combined pill, one tablet a day is usually taken for twenty-one days, then menstruation occurs, and the pills are resumed, taken on a twenty-eight-day cycle. The 'mini-pill' is taken every day, at the same time each day, whether or not menstruation is taking place. It is important to discuss with a doctor or family planning clinic the type of method or pills to be taken; there are many brands and if one is not suitable another may be more so.

The pill is virtually totally effective if taken according to instructions. Its use does not interfere with lovemaking, and many women experience shorter and less painful periods with the combined pill. This type is also a reliable guide to when menstruation will occur. Periods are much more likely to be erratic with the 'mini-pill' and it is usually difficult to predict when menstruation will occur when taking this type of pill, especially in the first few months.

There are some disadvantages in taking oral contraceptives and it is not a safe or pleasant method for everyone, so medical advice must always be sought. Some women experience side effects, such as unwanted weight gain, headaches, and depression, and it is not suitable for those with certain medical histories such as varicose veins, blood clots, and gall bladder problems. Also, the pill may be forgotten, which reduces the efficiency of this method. Women who suffer from depression are often advised to take the progestogen-only 'mini pill' plus some vitamin B6 tablets to combat this problem.

There are various types of *IUDs* – intra-uterine devices (the coil or loop) – which can be used by women who have not had children. A small coil or shaped device is placed in the uterus by a family planning specialist and this affects the lining of the womb so a fertilized egg does not get implanted. Once it is in place it can be virtually forgotten except for periodic checks that it hasn't fallen out. This is a highly effective method but while many women find the IUD an ideal way to prevent conception others cannot tolerate this 'foreign body'. There can be heavy bleeding especially during the first few months after insertion and some women have very painful cramps. Only experience will tell you whether you are in the pro- or anti-IUD camp! When you decide you want to try to have a child, the loop is easily and quickly removed by a doctor or at the family planning clinic.

The diaphragm (cap) when used together with a spermicide is very effective. A thin rubber dome or cap, rather like a shallow saucer with an outer rubber-covered ring, is placed deep inside the vagina to cover the cervix (entrance to the womb) and prevent sperm reaching the uterus. Spermicidal jelly or cream placed on both sides of the cap before insertion kills or immobilizes sperm on contact. It must be fitted by a family planning specialist to ensure the correct size. It is placed in the vagina before lovemaking and has to be left in position for six to eight hours after intercourse. More spermicide, in the form of pessaries, has to be used for successive lovemaking. When removed it must be washed, dried, and put away until next time. There are no side effects and if used regularly, carefully, and always with spermicide, it offers good protection, especially when used in conjunction with a condom. It can interrupt lovemaking (it's best to put it in routinely every night) and some women find inserting it is aesthetically unpleasing.

Foams, creams and chemical barriers are spermicidal preparations in the form of small tablets or gel, with an applicator or aerosol, placed in the woman's vagina before intercourse to kill or immobilize sperm. While there are no side effects the failure risk of these when used alone is high, particularly so when not used correctly. They interrupt lovemaking and some women find they cause irritations. Contraceptive sponges are easier to use and can be bought at the chemist's counter. A sponge is placed high in the vagina and can be left in place for up to 12 hours. Sponges have a higher failure rate than a correctly used cap and spermicide.

A condom (sheath, protective, rubber or French letter) is a thin sheath placed over the man's erect penis immediately before he enters the woman's vagina to prevent semen entering the vagina. The man must take his penis out of the woman as soon as intercourse is over because the condom may slip off as his penis returns to its normal size. Most effective when used with a spermicide. A new sheath and more spermicide is used each time intercourse takes place. It can interfere with lovemaking and detract from sensations. Failures can happen due to puncture or slipping off in the vagina.

Withdrawal (or 'being careful') means the man removes his penis just before he climaxes, so sperm do not enter the woman's body. However, there are dangers – the man may leave it too late, a little drop of semen may escape without notice – and the act of intercourse is less enjoyable, especially for the woman. Not a method that is recommended either for safety or a satisfying sex life.

The rhythm method (safe period) is usually used only by those people who have a religious reason for not using other types of contraception. You must not have intercourse on days when pregnancy is possible, i.e. around the woman's ovulation date and you must allow four days on either side of that date. Although it reduces the chance of pregnancy, it is not a reliable method because the actual date of ovulation is not always easy to determine and may vary from month to month. It cuts down drastically on the days available for lovemaking. Advice, much more detail, and special temperature charts are available from family planning clinics and the Catholic Marriage Advisory Council.

Sterilization is not a method of contraception likely to be wanted by newly marrieds (except in medically necessary cases), and *abortion* should never be seen as an alternative method of contraception. Apart from any moral arguments on this subject, it only ends the present pregnancy and does not prevent future ones occurring. To have a termination can be a traumatic and emotional experience and repeated abortions can be physically harmful.

For most people, adequate contraception (birth control) is essential. Without it a young woman of about twenty could possibly have twenty or more babies in her procreative lifetime – and few would welcome that! For couples who plan to have a family in the future, it is essential to discuss this well before the wedding, for even one act of unprotected intercourse can result in an unplanned child. You should discuss together the various types and methods of birth control, and who is to take responsibility – or whether you take it in turns. If for religious reasons you cannot use any of the mechanical methods, it is essential to find out about the 'safe period' or rhythm method. Sex is a vital part of the marriage relationship, and if you are tense and constantly worrying about the possibility of getting pregnant you are not going to enjoy lovemaking.

35

The Honeymoon

Once you have set the date for the wedding you can start planning the honeymoon. There are so many possibilities of places to go, so your decision will be affected by cost – what you can afford and how much you both want to spend – and the sort of holiday you both imagine as being an ideal honeymoon. It isn't essential to go abroad on honeymoon. A few days spent relaxing in the luxury of a superb hotel (say a country house hotel) can be much more enjoyable than a cheap package holiday somewhere hot.

How far do you want to travel – home or abroad? Do you want to be at a seaside resort or to be out in the country? Do you want plenty of locally available entertainment, to do lots of sightseeing, to be busy in a city or laze about in the sun? How important is the weather? If you want sun in December you will have to travel a long distance.

The timing of the wedding and type of reception you plan to have can affect whether you leave on holiday from the reception or whether you stay to the end of the party and spend the first night after the wedding in a hotel not far away. If you are planning to travel some distance, checking into a 'halfway house' hotel for the night or weekend is probably preferable anyway. For safety's sake you may not want to drive too far – being high on excitement not to mention champagne – but you'll probably be quite tired and welcome a break, to be alone together and relax before dealing with the hassles of travelling, especially if you are planning to travel a long distance.

The few months leading up to the wedding will have been pretty tiring, and you may be coming back to a new house and lots of work, so a busy or energetic type of holiday may not be ideal for a honeymoon. The other extreme of going somewhere ultra quiet could leave you both a bit bored and irritated with each other especially if the weather isn't good.

If you're happy about everyone knowing you're on honeymoon, let the hotel know at the time of booking. Many hotels give special discounts or free champagne and flowers. Special honeymoon travel trips, package tours and hotel arrangements are advertized in magazines and the press and various travel leaflets are available listing romantic honeymoon spots and hotels with four-poster beds or honeymoon suites. You can make the booking arrangements yourselves, or leave it to a travel agent. If using an agent, choose a reputable one, preferably one you or your friends have used before and can recommend.

Part of the fun of going away is reading the travel brochures together, and once you've decided on the holiday location, reading up on the place you're to visit and the area around it. Traditionally, the travel plans are the groom's responsibility, but planning is a lot of fun when it's shared.

Think about the type of clothes you'll need well in advance – you won't want to be dashing out to the shops for last-minute holiday shopping when there are so many other things to do and check for the wedding itself. Bear in mind the type of holiday you will be having and what the weather could be like, and pack accordingly. Too much heavy luggage is a nuisance when travelling especially if you are flying, so travel as light as possible. Humping heavy cases around makes you ratty and tired – the extra time and thought put in to careful packing will prove worthwhile.

With all the planning in the months leading up to the wedding you'll be used to making lists – make one for your honeymoon packing, too. This ensures you won't forget anything and stops you packing too many unwanted extras. Sit down quietly and imagine how you'll be spending this very special holiday. Make a note of the clothes you are likely to need for the various activities and places you plan to see.

Try to buy crease-resistant clothes and make good use of separates that will mix and match. A few basics that interchange with each other are the mainstay of holiday wear.

Choose a good-looking suitcase that will hold everything you want to take and still leave a bit of space for souvenirs and holiday buys. Before packing, spread out everything you plan to take. Check that you really do need everything, and that the clothes and accessories co-ordinate.

The things you will need first on arrival should be packed last – you won't want to unpack the entire suitcase just to find a bikini. Ideally, especially when flying, toiletries should be kept separate from clothes. Lightweight plastic travel packs of everything in liquid or cream form are preferable to bottles, and reduce the size and weight of toiletries. Shoes are heavy, so only take the ones you know you'll need. Never pack money, travellers cheques or a camera in your main suitcase.

A small overnight bag containing make-up, toiletries, a lightweight dress and a spare pair of undies is useful insurance just in case your luggage goes astray. You'll want to buy things on holiday, and if you are going abroad there'll be duty frees, so pack a lightweight shopping or carrybag to hold everything in case you buy too much! Pack a few plastic carrier bags, too, for damp swimwear and dirty laundry.

Just to jog your memory, here's a short check-list of things you could need: casual clothes, beachwear, evening clothes, sports wear and sports equipment, lingerie, accessories, shoes, contraceptives, cosmetics and sun creams, a basic first-aid kit, camera and film, hairdryer (and adaptor).

Other essentials not to be forgotten, of course, are the travel tickets and reservation vouchers as well as travellers' cheques, credit cards, foreign currency, passport and any necessary visas. If you are travelling to exotic places, inoculations or injections may be required. Check whether these are necessary and if they are, have them well in advance.

You can travel on honeymoon with your existing passport in your maiden name. If you want a passport in your married name you will have to apply to the Passport Office in good time before the wedding, but they will not give you the passport until you are actually married. You can, however, arrange for the new passport to be sent to the vicar or minister who is conducting the ceremony and who will hold it in safekeeping until you are legally Mr and Mrs. If you do not need the passport for travel immediately, you can keep your existing valid passport and simply have the name on it changed when convenient. A form from the post office has to be completed and sent, together with the passport and your marriage certificate to the Passport Office, Clive House, Petty France, London SW1. There is a charge for the alteration to be made.

A honeymoon is simply a very special holiday, but it can have its tensions and problems. Don't be too surprised or upset if everything does not match up to your fantasies and expectations. If it is the first time you've been on holiday together, there are many adjustments to be made. Most people have horror stories to tell and later laugh about their honeymoon experiences. Sex can be disappointing, and you may get bored and irritated with each other.

One couple described their honeymoon as 'shock therapy'. Try to relax, deal with the shocks and the nice surprises as they come, don't panic – and remember you've got many years ahead in which you'll adjust, get to know each other and have good sex as well as to learn to love his or her funny habits!

36

The Changing Times

Today, most women can choose to marry the man they love; our ancestors were not so lucky. In the Middle Ages, for example, not only did women have no legal rights over their own property, but their husband was chosen for them to ensure the property remained in suitable hands – or to gain political power or enlarge estates or kingdoms. Girls growing up in a family of property were often betrothed virtually in their cradles and married in their early teens to men much older than themselves.

Marriage was heavily linked with property transactions for the 'upper classes' and women were seen as forms of property and 'necessary evils'. Marriages of convenience were still common in the eighteenth and nineteenth centuries. In 1882 the law was changed to allow women to keep their property after marriage.

In medieval times, most of the wedding ceremony took place in the church porch and only when the ring was safely on the finger could the couple enter the church and complete the ceremony.

White is always considered the 'traditional' colour of wedding dresses, the sign of purity, but this is a fairly recent idea dating back to the late eighteenth century. Long hair hanging down her back was an earlier sign of the bride's virginity.

The reception as we know it has a long history and was much more boisterous in earlier times. This was a joyous occasion and a perfect excuse for feasting, singing and dancing, often for days on end. Then there was the ceremony of 'putting the bride to bed', a tradition which lasted into the eighteenth century. She was undressed by female relatives and bridesmaids, who carefully extracted all the pins, and the groom's men fought hard for the silken garter ribbon which held up the bride's stockings – many a bride emerged bruised from that little exercise. The attendants then played a game throwing the stockings over their shoulders on the nuptial bed. This was supposed to ensure the success of their own marriages, as well as being fun.

During Oliver Cromwell's era, jollity at weddings was not expected and there were many fewer church weddings then, too. In the next century, privacy became the trend. Marriages often took place at home, in ordinary clothes, followed by an informal meal and perhaps a honeymoon not far away, for travelling was a dangerous occupation. The couple were often accompanied by a female relative or stayed with friends.

The late seventeenth and early eighteenth centuries were notorious for Fleet weddings, so called because they took place around the Fleet debtors' prison area and were conducted by defrocked and fake clergy. Many an heiress was robbed of her fortune in this manner. Lord Hardwicke's 1754 Act of Parliament put an end to these rackets by setting rules and regulations for the conducting of marriages – and this Act formed the basis of the laws governing marriages in England and Wales today.

Towards the end of the eighteenth century the wedding ceremony and all that went with it was highlighted. Here began the fashion for marrying in white with a veil. As the nineteenth century began, the fashion was for white and gold with every lady aspiring to resemble the classical Greek statue. Later, wedding dresses were often made with two bodices, one for the wedding and one, less modest, for evening wear. These were worn until considered out of fashion. The skirt was probably then cut up to provide christening robes.

The nineteenth century was a fashion-conscious time, later dictated by the gowns of the young Queen Victoria. As she grew in size, attempting to hide her many pregnancies, the fashion silhouette grew more rounded. Crinolines were in vogue, then the bustle. It was only in the 1920s that the real shape of the body became acceptable (except for the bust!). The Victorian and Edwardian bridal fashions demanded crinolines and bustles all covered with innumerable petticoats. There were layers and layers of clothing. Stockings were made of silk for the rich, cotton for the poor, who knitted their own.

Today's bride receives wedding presents but in the past the bride's parents also gave presents (called wedding favours) to the guests. They were often gloves, bunches of ribbon or small bouquets. It was reported that favours of ribbon, lace and orange blossom were given at Queen Victoria's wedding in 1840.

There was one invention that changed the look of wedding dresses – the sewing machine – and made a splendid white wedding more of a possibility for the masses. In past years the well-brought-up young lady was expected to be accomplished at sewing and needlework, spending her days sewing the kind of fine seam that would leave us breathless with admiration.

Wedding dresses were usually made at home, either by the bride herself and the female members of the family or by a sewing woman, who would come in and sew all day for a pittance. Whole trousseaux would be made in this way, and were expected to last a lifetime. Various articles of underwear and household linens were made or ordered in dozens (or by the gross, according to status).

Because Britain (and Europe) was an entirely male-dominated society before World War One, women's struggle for emancipation was particularly long and hard. There were even instances of husbands selling their wives. In the 1850s, enough women banded together to collect 26,000 signatures to place before Parliament in an attempt to get a better deal.

Women were not considered to have minds, to be capable of rational thought, so they had to 'catch their man' through their beauty. Ladies' magazines of the Victorian era had plenty of advice, hints and warnings about behaviour, etiquette and fashion. Many fashion plates of the time gave detailed views of the front and back views of wedding dresses. Ribbons, bows, orange blossom and lovers knots were all favourite decorations for the dress, as was lace. Fashionable weddings were reported around the turn of the century, a time when women were gaining more freedom of action.

White weddings were the accepted form for brides of the upper classes, though for the lower and middle classes coloured 'Sunday best' dresses continued to be worn as they had for many centuries. To wear white proved that the girl's father was rich enough to provide a dress for her that was to be worn on one single occasion. This trend grew as the money from industry grew and 'affluence' began to overtake 'nobility' in the society fashion stakes.

In the mid-1920s fashion took on a very different look. The great designer Coco Chanel kept her boyish look for day but her bridal gowns were feminine and simple. The feminine woman returned in the 1930s, personified by Greta Garbo. Wedding dresses of this period were of simple well-cut design, worn with a small coronet on the back of a short hairstyle to create the effect of height and gracefulness.

With the approach of yet another war, fashion became more romantic with upswept hairstyles and the return of the Victorian fashion influence. Hats were popular and the dirndl skirt was a favourite on wedding dresses. The war years of make-do-and-mend stretched everyone's imagination to create a special dress for a wedding. Creativity and ingenuity were essential.

The 1950s saw full skirts and layers of petticoats but for the young of the 1960s the decline of fashion rules meant 'anything goes' in terms of fashion trends – there were minis, maxis, trouser suits, boots, painted faces, all of which were translated into wedding fashions. Freedom ruled, but while the mini wedding dress was popular, so still was the conventional long white dress with veil and bouquet, the traditional church wedding and reception.

And so it is today, when we see 'traditional white' still very popular with a trend to old lace and Victoriana, all feminine and fragile. Wedding dresses generally bear little relation to the fashion of the day but more often resemble those of an earlier generation.

Women have gained much more personal freedom this century, but perhaps for just one day in our lives we love to hark back to the days of being cosseted, the centre of attention, and all the fashion frippery of an era that at least seems so much more romantic.

37

The Bride's A–Z of Her Wedding

A is for Arrangements for your wedding. The most important day of your life takes a lot of organizing and you should allow yourself several months to arrange everything comfortably from A–Z. But of course the bigger the wedding, the more time it will take and if you're choosing a popular time of year and a well-known reception venue you can start booking anything up to a year beforehand. When you've named the day it's never too early to get the wedding wheels turning.

B is for Banns which are called in church for three consecutive Sundays before the wedding date . . . and for *Bridesmaids* – how many and who is the choice you have to make. You should discuss what they'll wear when you're thinking of your own dress and decide whether you're going to pay for their dresses or whether they'll contribute . . . and for *Best Man* who will be chosen by your fiancé. The best man has a number of duties including looking after the ring before it's placed on your finger, reading out telegrams – and making sure that the groom gets to the wedding on time!

C is for Church wedding, the date for which is the first thing to organize (and this is the case with all traditional weddings). So it's off to see the minister, priest or rabbi to arrange the time, date and also other details like bells, flowers and music. If you choose to get married in a church outside your local parish, you can be put on the electoral role for six months before the wedding day, during which time you'll be expected to attend the church services, regularly . . . and for the *Cake* you'll need to give a baker several weeks' notice telling him what colour (not everyone wants white), how many tiers and what decorations you want. Often the caterers of your wedding will organize the cake and will supply a stand too . . . and for *Caterers* because if you're just hiring a hall and you don't want to do this work yourselves, local caterers (and it's very important that they're recommended) will supply the food to your needs – in your own home too if that's what you decide. Contact them once you've booked a hall or decided on a home reception . . . and for *Cars* which should be hired from a local and reliable firm several weeks beforehand . . . and for *Confetti*, although some ministers aren't too pleased when it's thrown around the church grounds so check first and warn friends if that's the case.

D is for Dress and if you're having it made for you, book a recommended dressmaker as one of your priorities. If you're buying one, give yourself plenty of time to see what's around (and be careful not to buy something far too summery for a winter wedding or vice versa) and to allow time for any alterations which might be needed.

E is for Etiquette which covers just about everything from how invitations should be written to who pays for what and who performs what task. How much of this you want to comply with is entirely a matter of choice.

F is for Flowers which includes your own and the bridesmaids' plus any others you may want. Your bouquet should be ordered a few weeks in advance from a local and reputable florist to arrive at your home on the morning of the wedding day. Button-holes are the best man's responsibility . . . and for *Family Planning*, so if you haven't already done so, arrange for an appointment with your local family planning clinic or doctor at least a month before you get married.

G is for Guests and you should sort out with both sets of parents the number of relatives they want to ask, so that you know exactly who you plan to invite.

H is for Honeymoon and because people book up their holidays so far in advance, your honeymoon should be booked at least six months in advance to get what you want. If you tell the travel agent you'll be honey-mooners, some companies arrange for flowers and champagne . . . and for *Hair and Headdress* – when you've got your headdress take it along to your hairdresser so that he or she can experiment with hairstyles.

I is for Invitations which should be sent out six weeks before the day so that people have time to reply. When you have finalized dates and places for wedding and reception you should order the invitations from a good stationers if you want them printed.

J is for June weddings which are immensely popular (as are summer and Bank Holiday weddings such as Easter ones), so if it's a 'moon in June' wedding you want, book the church and reception as far in advance as you can. Twelve months may not be too soon in some areas for popular times of the year.

K is for Keeping as cool, calm and clear-headed as possible while making all these arrangements, though you may feel like pulling your hair out at times.

L is for Lists – keep making them, of all the things you have to do, and tick items systematically when they've been seen to. With so many important matters at stake, it's essential to be efficient.

M is for Menus which you'll sort out with the caterers and arrange the most suitable meal or buffet according to your needs and cash . . . and for *Make-up* because you should know exactly how you want to look on your wedding day . . . and for *Money* which will probably be constantly in your thoughts while you're arranging everything. It would be advisable to keep an accounts book so you can see where every penny goes! . . . as well as *Mother* and *Mother-in-law* who can be very helpful in taking over much of the organizing of the wedding. Give them a hug of thanks and appreciation.

N is for Night – the First One, that is. If you're going to spend your first night in a hotel try to arrange it a month or so beforehand. If you're going away book a place near the airport, ferry or station – and don't tell anyone where it is (apart from your partner, of course!) . . . and for *Name* – don't forget to inform the relevant people like the tax office, bank, credit card companies that you're changing yours (if you are).

O is for Organization – the keyword in making your wedding day run smoothly.

P is for Presents – and it's better to make several copies of wedding lists for friends and family than to risk having the same gift from four people. Alternatively, many large department stores have a Brides List – your guests can select what to buy for you when they shop at the store. It's a nice custom for you to buy a present – a small trinket – for your bridesmaids. Make sure you have someone list the presents and the names of those who gave them as they arrive: it makes it much easier to write thank-you notes later . . . and for the *Photographer* who should be booked up well in advance of the wedding date. Go to one who's been recommended to you – good pictures of your special day are so important . . . and for *Parties*, both of the hen and stag variety which are great, but make sure you both have them a couple of nights before the event, for obvious reasons . . . and for *Passports* – in fact, you don't need to change this, even though it does have your maiden name on it, until it reaches the expiry date. However, some brides don't want to go away under separate names and if that's the case you should apply for a new passport when arranging your honeymoon.

Q is for Quotations – you should do plenty of shopping around when it comes to organizing this very expensive occasion, especially in the case of hotels, photographers, caterers, cars and so on, to get the very best value for money.

R is for Register office wedding – you should notify the registrar for your area that you want to get married. For marriage by licence, you can be married after one clear day has elapsed (so long as you have a fifteen-day residential qualification). However, taking it for granted that you don't want to tie the knot in such a hurry, once you've given notice to marry it remains sound for three months . . . and for *Reception* which could be large or small, in a pub or restaurant, hall, hotel or at home. You should give yourself plenty of time to organize this so you can find just what you want and can arrange it down to the finest detail, i.e: the food, the music, the drinks, flowers for decor-ation, the table plan, the toastmaster and so on. How elaborate or how simple depends on finances and exactly what you would like most. If you are having a large wedding and book a hall with caterer or hotel, the details as mentioned here are usually sorted out by them and you decide together exactly what you want. If you decide on a hotel, it might be an idea to have a meal there some time before choosing finally so you can get some idea of their standards. Once you decide on and book a wedding date, you should set about organizing your reception . . . and for *Ring* – yours and his should be ordered a few months in advance if being specially made so you can discuss designs and make sure they fit properly. However, if you know what you want and it's a simple ring sold in High Street jewellers' shops then giving yourself six weeks or so should be fine and allows time for fitting alterations.

S is for Speeches – brides usually get out of this one! Your groom, your best man and your father or other members of your family make toasts and speeches – long, short, funny or otherwise!

T is for Trousseau – for lovely nighties, going-away and honeymoon clothes. Allow yourself a good few weeks so you don't find yourself buying clothes in a last-minute panic and buying things you don't feel one hundred per cent happy in. Don't dash about in the lunch hour and buy in a hurry. Since shopping for your trousseau is very important, why not take your mum or a friend with you so that you have a second opinion if you're not sure about certain garments? . . . and for *Thank-you letters* for presents which can either be written as they arrive or sent shortly after the honeymoon.

U is for Ushers – usually three for formal church weddings. They arrive at the church first and direct guests to their seats, give out service sheets at the door of the church and help to organize lifts from the place of ceremony to the reception.

V is for the Vows you'll be making – and that's what it's all about. . . .

W is for Witness – you'll need two for register office weddings and they can be friends, or even strangers. In church weddings often the chief bridesmaid and best man are chosen to sign the register as witnesses.

X is for Crossing your fingers that it all goes well.

Y is for You – it's *your* day so give yourself plenty of time to get everything and yourself ready and leave nothing to chance. And if it all gets a bit too much at times don't despair, just try to keep calm and remember that once it's all over you'll be starting out on a great future with your new husband.

Z is for Zest – you'll need plenty of it during the months before your Big Day. You'll need it for final checks with florists, church, reception, caterers, photographers, car firms and so on to make sure everyone's got it right.

Then all that remains for you to do is to actually get down to the very rewarding business of getting married to the man you love.

Countdown to Your Wedding

Five or more months before the wedding

- Determine your budget with your fiancé and parents. Decide whether your wedding will be formal or informal, and where the ceremony will take place.
- Visit and make arrangements with the minister or superintendent registrar of your district who will be conducting your wedding and set the date for the ceremony.
- Make a plan for the reception, see caterers, get estimates, book the venue as soon as possible.
- Draw up a list for wedding invitations, in consultation with your fiancé's family.
- Decide on bridesmaids, best man, ushers and attendants – and ask them!
- Decide on a colour scheme for the wedding.
- Shop for ideas for your wedding dress and attendants' attire, or arrange to have them made.
- Plan the men's wear, especially if the wedding is formal.
- Choose and book a professional photographer.
- Book hire cars.
- See a florist.

- Discuss your honeymoon destination and book as soon as possible in advance.
- Plan your future home and furnishings.

Three to five months before the wedding

- Finalize travel plans and ensure your honeymoon is booked and confirmed. Check if visas or vaccinations will be required. Organize a new passport in your married name.
- Decide on your budget for a trousseau, and begin shopping for it.
- Order your wedding stationery – invitations, reply cards, service sheets, personalized matchbooks, place cards for the reception, cake boxes, serviettes, writing paper, how-to-get-there maps, etc.
- Compile your wedding present list and/or register with a brides' list at a local store.
- Look at wedding rings.
- Help your mother choose her dress.
- Discuss colour scheming and co-ordinating colours with all members of the wedding party, male and female.
- Consult the minister about music for the wedding and any special prayers or readings you wish to have. See the organist, choir master and bell ringers.

Two months before the wedding

- Finalize the guest list. Write and post wedding invitations.
- Plan the recording and display of wedding gifts.

- Write thank-you letters as presents are received.
- Record acceptances and refusals to the invitations as they come in.
- Check that the wedding clothes you ordered are in preparation.
- Agree the choice of flowers with the florist.
- Decide on presents for your attendants and order or buy them.
- Arrange your wedding cake and liaise with caterers for the reception.
- Make an appointment and visit the family planning centre or doctor. See your dentist.
- Make sure your future home is organized.
- Book hotel rooms for out of town guests, if required.
- Buy the wedding ring(s) if you have not already done so.
- Get the marriage licence organized.
- Arrange any extra signs or parking facilities required for the reception.

One month before the wedding

- Talk to your hairdresser and plan the style for the wedding. Take your veil with you. Book an early appointment for the day of your wedding.
- Have a final fitting for the wedding dress.
- Make sure your wedding shoes are comfortable.
- Prepare a newspaper announcement of your wedding.
- Arrange a seating plan for the reception and see to place cards.

- Plan arrangements for attendants on the wedding day – where they will gather, dress, eat, etc.
- Calculate how many wedding cake boxes you will require.
- Try to give a final number of reception guests to the caterers.
- Finalize your going-away clothes. List everything you need to pack.
- Arrange for the name changes on bank cards, credit cards, savings accounts, etc. and inform the tax office and national insurance office, plus any other relevant officials.
- Make any moving arrangements for your new home.
- Check your fiancé has made all his arrangements for the wedding – hire of clothing for himself, best man, usher, etc.
- Go to church to hear your banns read.
- Check with the minister about the timing of the rehearsal, and inform everyone concerned.

One week before the wedding

- Make final checks on cake, catering, transport, photography, flowers, dresses, etc.
- Collect your wedding dress if not already done so.
- Try it on.
- Have a rehearsal of the wedding.
- Make sure you have everything for the honeymoon.
- Confirm arrangements for having your dress and his suit taken care of after the reception.

- Take your bridesmaids out to lunch or have a girls' night out. Give them their presents.
- Check the car is in good running order.
- Go to the hairdresser and practise your make up.
- Try to slow down! Have a cosseting beauty treatment.

On the day

- Sleep in. Have a good breakfast!
- Get hair and make-up done.
- Make sure going-away clothes, and luggage, have been delivered to the reception venue.
- Get dressed – take plenty of time.
- Put engagement ring on right hand.
- Hug (and thank) your parents.

Appendix II
Arrangement Planner

Attendants

Maid of Honour/Chief Bridesmaid

Name _____

Address _____

_____

Telephone _____

Dress size _____   Shoe size _____

Head size _____

Notes _____

_____

_____

_____

_____

_____

Best Man

Name _____

Address _____

_____

Jacket size_____   Shoe size_____

Trousers: waist_____   outside leg_____

              inside leg _____

Shirt: neck size _____   sleeve length_____

Hat size_____

Notes_____

_____

_____

Bride's Father

Jacket size_____   Shoe size_____

Trousers: waist_____   outside leg_____

              inside leg _____

Shirt: neck size _____   sleeve length_____

Hat size_____

Notes_____

_____

_____

Bridesmaid

Name _____

Address _____

_____

Telephone _____

Dress size_____ Shoe size _____

Head size_____

Notes _____

_____

_____

Bridesmaid

Name _____

Address _____

_____

Telephone _____

Dress size_____ Shoe size _____

Head size_____

Notes _____

_____

_____

Bridesmaid

Name _____

Address _____

_____

Telephone _____

Dress size _____ Shoe size _____

Head size _____

Notes _____

_____

_____

Bridesmaid

Name _____

Address _____

_____

Telephone _____

Dress size _____ Shoe size _____

Head size _____

Notes _____

_____

_____

Chief Usher

Name _____

Address _____

_____

Telephone _____

Notes _____

_____

_____

_____

_____

Usher

Name _____

Address _____

_____

Telephone _____

Notes _____

_____

_____

_____

_____

Usher

Name _____

Address _____

_____

Telephone _____

Notes _____

_____

_____

_____

_____

Usher

Name _____

Address _____

_____

Telephone _____

Notes _____

_____

_____

_____

_____

At the ceremony

Vicar/Minister/Registrar

Name _____

Address _____

_____

Telephone _____

Notes_____

_____

_____

_____

Church/Chapel/Register Office
where we will be married:

_____

_____

_____

_____

Organist

Name_____

Address _____

_____

Telephone _____

Notes_____

_____

Choir Master

Name _____

Address _____

_____

Telephone _____

Notes _____

_____

Services

Bridal wear

Name _____

Address _____

_____

Telephone _____

Person to contact _____

Notes _____

_____

_____

_____

Men's formal wear

Name _____

Address _____

_____

Telephone _____

Person to contact _____

Notes _____

_____

_____

_____

Dressmaker

Name _____

Address _____

_____

Telephone _____

Hairdresser

Name _____

Address _____

_____

Telephone _____

Make-up artist/Colour consultant

Name _____

Address _____

_____

Telephone _____

Caterers

Name _____

Address _____

_____

Telephone _____

Person to contact _____

Notes _____

_____

Bakery

Name _____

Address _____

_____

Telephone _____

Person to contact _____

Notes _____

_____

Photographer

Name _____

Address _____

_____

Telephone _____

Person to contact _____

Notes _____

_____

Car hire/transport

Name _____

Address _____

_____

Telephone _____

Person to contact _____

Notes _____

_____

Hire of equipment

Name _____

Address _____

_____

Telephone _____

Person to contact _____

Notes _____

_____

Music/Band/Disco

Name _____

Address _____

_____

Telephone _____

Person to contact _____

Notes _____

_____

Florist

Name _____

Address _____

_____

Telephone _____

Person to contact _____

Notes _____

_____

Stationers

Name _____

Address _____

_____

Telephone _____

Person to contact _____

Notes _____

_____

Travel Agent

Name _____

Address _____

_____

Telephone _____

Person to contact _____

Notes _____

_____

Dress details

The bridal dress

Neckline _____ Waistline _____

Sleeve style _____ Skirt style _____

Colour _____ Fabric _____

Headdress _____ Veil _____

Train _____ Shoes _____

Details of flowers/bouquet _____

Bridesmaids' dresses

Dress style _____

Colour _____ Fabric _____

Other details _____

Men's attire

Groom_____

Best man _____ Ushers_____

Bride's father_____

The women in the party

Bride's mother_____

Groom's mother _____

Bride's grandparents_____

Groom's grandparents_____

Planning the ceremony

Readings for the service _____

_____

_____

_____

_____

Special prayers_____

_____

_____

_____

_____

Music _____

_____

_____

_____

_____

_____

Hymns _____

_____

_____

_____

_____

Planning the flowers

My bouquet contains _____

_____

The colours are _____

My attendants' flowers are_____

_____

The bride's mother _____

The groom's mother _____

Grandparents _____

Buttonholes for the men _____

The groom's buttonhole is_____

The altar will be decorated with _____

At the church, arrangements will contain _____

_____

_____

At the reception there will be _____

Notes_____

_____

_____

_____

_____

_____

The guest list

Make index cards – one card for each person or family invited – which contain the following information:

Name _____

Address _____

_____

Telephone _____

Date invitation sent_____

Date reply received_____

Acceptance?_____

Number attending _____

Date wedding present received _____

Present _____

Date thank-you letter sent _____

Planning the reception

Seating for the top table: *Guest tables:*

_____   1 _____

_____

_____   2 _____

The menu: _____

_____   3 _____

_____

_____   4 _____

The drinks: _____

_____   5 _____

_____

_____   6 _____

Music: _____

_____   7 _____

_____

_____   8 _____

Notes: _____ _____

_____ 9 _____

_____ _____

_____ 10 _____

_____ _____

Planning the honeymoon

The town and country _____

The hotel _____

Our wedding night will be spent at _____

Travel arrangements _____

Passport numbers _____

Immunization needed? _____

Places to see _____

_____

_____

Things to do: _____

Things to pack: _____

_____

_____

Travel tickets and vouchers _____

Airport/station _____

Foreign currency _____

Any visas required?_____

Travellers' cheques _____

Car hire_____

Notes:_____

_____

Your Wedding Budget Planner

Reception

Hire of hall _____ £

Catering/food _____ £

Alcohol _____ £

Soft drinks _____ £

Coffee and tea _____ £

Wedding cake _____ £

Flowers for reception _____ £

Candles _____ £

Decorations _____ £

Hire of equipment _____ £

Tips _____ £

Music _____ £

Extras _____ £

_____

Total £

Photography

Engagement picture _____ £

Photography at wedding ___ £

Photography at reception __ £

Album _____ £

Duplicates for family _____ £

Extras _____ £

_____

Total £

Gifts

Groom's wedding gift _____ £

Bridesmaids' gifts _____ £

Groom's wedding ring _____ £

Best man's present _____ £

Gifts for ushers _____ £

Gift for parents _____ £

_____

Total £

Miscellaneous

Sound recording of wedding £

Videotape/film of wedding _ £

Hotel for wedding night ___ £

Transport to honeymoon
     departure point _____ £

Cost of honeymoon hotel __ £

Train/air tickets _____ £

Car hire _____ £

Petrol _____ £

_____

Total £

Engagement party

Engagement ring _____ £

Invitations _____ £

Caterer _____ £

Food _____ £

Drinks _____ £

Music _____ £

Hire of venue _____ £

Hire of equipment _____ £

Flowers _____ £

_____

Total £

Stationery

Press announcements _____ £

Invitations _____ £

Thank-you cards or paper __ £

Serviettes _____ £

Match books _____ £

Place cards _____ £

Cake boxes _____ £

Service sheets _____ £

Postage _____ £

_____

Total £

Clothes

Wedding dress _____ £

Underskirt _____ £

Headdress _____ £

Veil _____ £

Shoes _____ £

Tights _____ £

Gloves _____ £

Lingerie _____ £

Going-away outfit _____ £

_____

Total £

Clothes

Special honeymoon clothes _ £

Bridesmaids' dresses _____ £

Bridesmaids' accessories ___ £

Pageboy's clothes _____ £

Mother's outfit _____ £

Father's outfit _____ £

Hire of groom's morning
   dress or cost of suit _____ £

Other hire charges _____ £

Cosmetics _____ £

Hairdresser _____ £

Extras _____ £

_____

Total £

Wedding

Church/Register Office fees _ £

Licence _____ £

Music: choir _____ £

Music: organist _____ £

Bellringers _____ £

Flowers for church _____ £

Bride's bouquet _____ £

Bridesmaids' bouquets ____ £

Flower girl's posy _____ £

Corsage for mother _____ £

Buttonholes _____ £

Hire cars _____ £

Wedding ring _____ £

Ribbons & decorations ____ £

Extras _____ £

_____

Total £

Bestselling Women's Fiction

☐ A Better World Than This	Marie Joseph	£2.95
☐ The Stationmaster's Daughter	Pamela Oldfield	£2.95
☐ The Lilac Bus	Maeve Binchy	£2.50
☐ The Golden Urchin	Madeleine Brent	£2.95
☐ The Temptress	Jude Deveraux	£2.95
☐ The Sisters	Pat Booth	£3.50
☐ Erin's Child	Sheelagh Kelly	£3.99
☐ The Ladies of Missalonghi	Colleen McCullough	£2.50
☐ Seven Dials	Claire Rayner	£2.50
☐ The Indiscretion	Diana Stainforth	£3.50
☐ Satisfaction	Rae Lawrence	£3.50

Prices and other details are liable to change

ARROW BOOKS, BOOKSERVICE BY POST, PO BOX 29, DOUGLAS, ISLE OF MAN, BRITISH ISLES

NAME..

ADDRESS...

....

....

Please enclose a cheque or postal order made out to Arrow Books Ltd. for the amount due and allow the following for postage and packing.

U.K. CUSTOMERS: Please allow 22p per book to a maximum of £3.00.

B.F.P.O. & EIRE: Please allow 22p per book to a maximum of £3.00

OVERSEAS CUSTOMERS: Please allow 22p per book.

Whilst every effort is made to keep prices low it is sometimes necessary to increase cover prices at short notice. Arrow Books reserve the right to show new retail prices on covers which may differ from those previously advertised in the text or elsewhere.

Bestselling Fiction

☐ Saudi	Laurie Devine	£2.95
☐ Lisa Logan	Marie Joseph	£2.50
☐ The Stationmaster's Daughter	Pamela Oldfield	£2.95
☐ Duncton Wood	William Horwood	£3.50
☐ Aztec	Gary Jennings	£3.95
☐ The Pride	Judith Saxton	£2.99
☐ Fire in Heaven	Malcolm Bosse	£3.50
☐ Communion	Whitley Strieber	£3.50
☐ The Ladies of Missalonghi	Colleen McCullough	£2.50
☐ Skydancer	Geoffrey Archer	£2.50
☐ The Sisters	Pat Booth	£3.50
☐ No Enemy But Time	Evelyn Anthony	£2.95

Prices and other details are liable to change

ARROW BOOKS, BOOKSERVICE BY POST, PO BOX 29, DOUGLAS, ISLE OF MAN, BRITISH ISLES

NAME...

ADDRESS...

....

....

Please enclose a cheque or postal order made out to Arrow Books Ltd. for the amount due and allow the following for postage and packing.

U.K. CUSTOMERS: Please allow 22p per book to a maximum of £3.00.

B.F.P.O. & EIRE: Please allow 22p per book to a maximum of £3.00

OVERSEAS CUSTOMERS: Please allow 22p per book.

Whilst every effort is made to keep prices low it is sometimes necessary to increase cover prices at short notice. Arrow Books reserve the right to show new retail prices on covers which may differ from those previously advertised in the text or elsewhere.